Early praise for *Functional Web Development with Elixir, OTP, and Phoenix*

A must-have for new Elixir programmers ready to take on modern web development with the unique features of the platform. Lance gently guides readers through complex topics using fun, digestible examples. From OTP to proper Phoenix architecture, this book takes you step by step from the basics to building your own powerful, real-time applications.

➤ **Chris McCord**
   Author of the Phoenix Framework

What makes this book important and unique is the fact that it focuses more on development practices and less on technology mechanics. I recommend this book to anyone who wants to build production systems with Elixir and Phoenix.

➤ **Saša Jurić**
   Software Developer, Aircloak

Every Elixir developer should buy and read Lance's book. There are a lot of questions in the rapidly growing Elixir community about how to structure apps with Phoenix and OTP, and Lance provides compelling and thoughtful answers. The Islands app that the reader builds throughout the book isn't simply an app to learn functional web development; it's the blueprint for correctly building out almost any Elixir app.

➤ **Ben Marx**
   Lead Engineer, Bleacher Report

For many people, their first experience with Elixir is in the context of Phoenix, and when they build their app it's a "Phoenix app"—which is great! But eventually they hit a wall and want to learn more about OTP and Elixir. This is *the* book they should reach for, and the book I am sending to as many people as I can.

➤ **Jason Stiebs**
   Partner, RokkinCat LLC

Functional Web Development with Elixir, OTP, and Phoenix

Rethink the Modern Web App

Lance Halvorsen

The Pragmatic Bookshelf

Raleigh, North Carolina

Many of the designations used by manufacturers and sellers to distinguish their products are claimed as trademarks. Where those designations appear in this book, and The Pragmatic Programmers, LLC was aware of a trademark claim, the designations have been printed in initial capital letters or in all capitals. The Pragmatic Starter Kit, The Pragmatic Programmer, Pragmatic Programming, Pragmatic Bookshelf, PragProg and the linking *g* device are trademarks of The Pragmatic Programmers, LLC.

Every precaution was taken in the preparation of this book. However, the publisher assumes no responsibility for errors or omissions, or for damages that may result from the use of information (including program listings) contained herein.

Our Pragmatic books, screencasts, and audio books can help you and your team create better software and have more fun. Visit us at *https://pragprog.com*.

The team that produced this book includes:

Publisher: Andy Hunt
VP of Operations: Janet Furlow
Managing Editor: Brian MacDonald
Supervising Editor: Jacquelyn Carter
Indexing: Potomac Indexing, LLC
Copy Editor: Liz Welch
Layout: Gilson Graphics

For sales, volume licensing, and support, please contact *support@pragprog.com*.

For international rights, please contact *rights@pragprog.com*.

ISBN-13: 978-1-68050-243-5
Printed on acid-free paper.
Book version: P1.0—January 2018

Contents

Part II — Add OTP for Concurrency and Fault Tolerance

Part III — Add a Web Interface with Phoenix

Acknowledgments

Writing a book is so much more of a team effort than I would have imagined before I began. A whole host of people have made this book incalculably better than it would have been had I done everything alone.

The people who created the Elixir ecosystem have made this book possible. That goes back to the creators of Erlang, Joe Armstrong, Robert Virding, and Mike Williams. It continues on to the OTP team at Ericsson that codified the design patterns and Behaviours this book relies on so much. Finally, there's José Valim and Chris McCord, creators of Elixir and Phoenix, respectively.

I give a hearty thanks to the folks at the Pragmatic Bookshelf, who have been unfailingly kind, helpful, and supportive. I couldn't ask for a more generous organization to work with. And there are two people I need to thank in a more personal way.

I have joked that Jacquelyn Carter has the hardest job in the world. Besides her work as a development editor, she needs to be a coach, a project manager, and a psychologist. That's a lot of hats for one person to wear. I'm not sure how I would have made it through this whole process without her help.

Bruce Tate, the Elixir series editor, came through just when I needed him most with key inputs and insights that kept the book on track and on message. He also spoke to the community on behalf of the book at times when I could not.

Of course, all the technical reviewers shared their valuable insights and caught a host of mistakes before they made it into the final version. A hearty thanks to all of you—Brett Wise, Jason Stiebs, Wendy Smoak, Jeff Weiss, Matt Enlow, Sonny Scroggin, Chris Keathley, Erik Ketcham, Maurice Kelly, Mark Goody, Gabor Hajba, Kim Shrier, and Mitchell Henke.

Other reviewers went above and beyond, providing important feedback on tight deadlines and short notice. James Fish and Andrea Leopardi fit that bill, as did James Edward Gray II, who is working on his own book. Thank you all for your generosity and expertise.

I also need to give special thanks to Saša Jurić. He gave me so much of his time, sharing his experience and insights with discussion, code reviews, and good humor. The first part of this book would not be the same without these generous contributions.

I've saved my most heartfelt thanks for the person dearest to me on Earth, my wife Laura, whose patience and support mean the world to me.

Introduction

I've been building web applications for a long, long time, well before web frameworks existed. In those early days, a Perl script or two in an Apache cgi-bin directory and a couple of static HTML files were all you needed.

In the intervening years, web frameworks for both the front and back ends have become ubiquitous. This has been fantastic for the industry. The productivity gains are undeniable, and the consistency across applications allows us to onboard new developers more quickly.

But along with these gains have come some costs. The way we're commonly taught to use frameworks causes extremely tight coupling between the framework components and our business logic. Databases have gone from simply augmenting storage to dominating the way we model application domains.

Most people come to Elixir and Phoenix for the performance, and there's no question that the performance is fantastic. Personally, I see Elixir—especially the access it gives us to OTP—and Phoenix providing solid solutions to these long-standing problems without sacrificing any of the gains. I also see them opening up new possibilities—bringing back some of the benefits of statefulness that we've lost with the rise of HTTP.

Throughout this book we'll be building a web application together that shows what Elixir, OTP, and Phoenix can really do when used well together. But most of all, you'll have fun and learn things you can use to make the code for your day job or side projects more beautiful, easier to maintain, and a joy to work on.

Who This Book Is For

On a practical level, this book is for people who have some familiarity with Elixir and Phoenix, and who want to take that knowledge further. But there's a wider list for whom the ideas in this book will resonate.

For people who view OTP with a little trepidation, or for those who haven't quite mastered OTP Behaviours, this book will give you the confidence to use OTP in any application.

For people who have felt the sting of tight coupling between business logic and web frameworks, this book will show you a way out of that pain forever.

For people who feel constrained by traditional web development, you will learn new techniques and new ways to structure apps that will spark your imagination.

For people who are wondering what all the fuss is about with Elixir and Phoenix, you'll get a great taste of what makes people so excited. You just might become a convert!

Who This Book Is Not For

Readers looking for an introduction to Elixir or Phoenix would do well to begin with other resources.

We won't cover the basics of Elixir. I'll assume you know them before you begin.

If you need to get up to speed first, don't worry—we'll be here when you're ready. In the meantime, Dave Thomas's book, *Programming Elixir 1.3 [Tho16]*, is a great place to start.

The same is true for Phoenix. We will take a close look at channels and Presence, but you won't learn the rest of Phoenix here.

You should be able to follow along in this book without that information, but if you want to fill in the gaps, *Programming Phoenix [TV16]* by Chris McCord, Bruce Tate, and José Valim is the book to reach for.

About This Book

Throughout this book, we'll be building a game in distinct layers—from the bare essentials of the business logic to a web front end with stateful Phoenix channels.

The book is divided up into three sequential parts that parallel those layers. The first part lays the foundation, and each of the next two parts builds a new layer that depends on the one that came before.

If you're planning on implementing the game as you read, which is a great idea, you'll need to follow through the parts in order for the code to work.

If you're the sort of reader who likes to skip around, though, all is not lost. You can read the first few sections of any chapter—up until where we start to really implement the code—in any order, and they will still hold value.

Before we get to work in earnest, you'll read an overview of the whole book in Chapter 1, *Mapping Our Route*, on page 1.

Now let's see what each part has to offer.

Define the Functional Core in Elixir

We'll begin with only the most basic elements of Elixir—data structures, functions, and modules.

In Chapter 2, *Model Data and Behavior*, on page 9, we'll use data structures to model our domain entities. We'll define functions that work with these data structures to establish the business logic of the game. We'll also define modules to organize these functions and keep the code legible and easy to maintain.

In Chapter 3, *Manage State with a State Machine*, on page 43, we'll build a purely functional finite state machine to manage the game over time and enforce the rules. We'll proceed the same way we did in Chapter 2, with a data structure, multiple clauses of a single function, and a module to hold them all.

Add OTP for Concurrency and Fault Tolerance

This is where we'll introduce OTP to provide concurrency, parallelism, and fault tolerance.

In Chapter 4, *Wrap It Up in a GenServer*, on page 65 we'll build a GenServer module to contain the business logic and state machine we built in Part 1. You'll learn how to spawn a new, long-lived process from this GenServer for each pair of players. That process will hold the state for their game as well as provide an interface to interact with it.

In Chapter 5, *Process Supervision for Recovery*, on page 97 we'll explore how to make our game resilient to failures large and small. We'll build a supervisor to watch over each game process and restart it if it crashes. You'll also see how to restore a game process's state after a crash and even after the whole BEAM, Erlang's virtual machine, crashes or restarts.

Add a Web Interface with Phoenix

With all the work we've done in the previous two parts, we'll finally be ready to build a web interface with Phoenix.

In Chapter 6, *Generate a New Web Interface with Phoenix*, on page 131 we'll create a new Phoenix project. You'll learn how OTP applications let us seamlessly integrate our work from the first two parts into this new Phoenix project as a dependency. Then we'll explore how we can call into that earlier work directly from different Phoenix components.

In Chapter 7, *Create Persistent Connections with Phoenix Channels*, on page 153 we'll focus on the stateful, persistent connections that Phoenix provides called channels. You'll learn how to use JavaScript functions in a browser to communicate directly over a channel with a specific game process on the server. We'll also explore how to use Phoenix Presence to keep track of which players are actually playing an individual game.

Online Resources

The code we'll develop is available at the Pragmatic Programmers site for this book. There's also a community forum and errata-submission form for you to ask questions, report any problems with the text, or make suggestions for future versions.[1]

---

1. https://pragprog.com/book/lhelph/functional-web-development-with-elixir-otp-and-phoenix

CHAPTER 1

Mapping Our Route

Welcome! We're about to go exploring, and it's going to be a blast. We're going to do what many of us say we love most—play with new languages, experiment with new techniques, and expand our understanding of writing software for the web. Whenever you go exploring, it's important to have a map, a good idea of where you're headed, and a plan for how you'll get there. That's what this chapter is all about.

Many early client-server systems were stateful. Servers kept working state in memory. They passed messages back and forth with their clients over persistent connections. Think of a banking system with a central mainframe and a dedicated terminal for each teller. This worked because the number of clients was small. Having fewer clients limited the system resources necessary to maintain those concurrent connections.

Then Tim Berners-Lee invented a new client-server system called the World Wide Web.

The web is an incredibly successful software platform. It's available almost everywhere on Earth, on virtually any device. As the web has grown and spread, so has HTTP. HTTP is a stateless protocol, so we think of web applications as stateless as well. This is an illusion. State is necessary for applications to do anything interesting, but instead of keeping it in memory on the server, we push it off into a database where it awaits the next request.

Offloading state to a database provides some real advantages. HTTP-based applications need to maintain temporary connections with clients only until they send a response, so they require far fewer resources to serve the same number of requests. Most languages can't muster the concurrency necessary to maintain enough persistent connections to be meaningful for a modern web application.

Going "stateless" has let us scale.

But statelessness comes at a cost. It introduces significant latency as applications need to make one or more trips to the database for the data to prepare a response. It makes the database a scaling bottleneck, and it habituates us to model data for databases rather than for application code.

Elixir offers more than enough concurrency to power stateful servers. Phoenix channels provide the conduit. A single Phoenix application can maintain persistent channel connections to hundreds of thousands or even millions of clients simultaneously. Those clients can all broadcast messages to each other, coordinated through the server. While processing those messages, the application remains snappy and responsive. Elixir and Phoenix provide a legitimate alternative to stateless servers capable of handling modern web traffic.

We're about to explore this new opportunity with a stateful application written in Elixir and a persistent Phoenix channel ready to connect it to any front-end application.

We'll do this by building a game called Islands. It may not be a top download on your favorite gaming platform, but it will be fun to play. Most importantly, you'll learn a lot by building it. Game developers have always pushed the web to the extreme. They've had to approach problems in novel ways to meet their performance needs. We'll be rethinking our approach as well, and what we'll learn will help us solve everyday business problems in radically improved ways.

We're going to tackle Islands in distinct parts. We'll start with a stateful game engine written in Elixir, and then we'll layer on a web interface with Phoenix.

We'll stop just short of building out a full front-end application—there won't be any new territory for us to cover.

We will include code for a demo front-end application with the code bundle for this book. Once you've built the full application, you'll be able to download those files and include them in the completed Phoenix project. That will allow you to play a demo game locally on your machine.

We're going to build Islands in a way you might not be used to, so let's get an idea of what lies ahead.

Lay the Foundation with Elixir

In Part 1, we'll begin by defining the data structures and logic of the game in pure Elixir. We won't use a database to store the game state, and we'll define our domain elements with native Elixir data structures instead of ORM models.

We will bring in a finite state machine to manage state transitions—like switching from one player's turn to the other, and moving from a game in progress to one player winning.

Building the game engine solely in Elixir solves a long-standing problem in web development, the tendency for framework code to completely entangle application logic so the two can't be easily separated. Without that separation, it's hard to reuse application logic in other contexts. As we build Islands, we won't even begin to work with the Phoenix framework until our game logic is complete.

In Part 2, we'll layer on OTP for concurrency and fault tolerance. We'll hold the data structures we've defined in the GenServer as state. Then we'll build a supervisor to monitor the GenServer and restart it with known, good state in the event of a crash.

By the time we're done with Parts 1 and 2, we'll have a fast, fault-tolerant game engine that can spin up a new GenServer for a game almost instantly. We'll be able to reuse it with any interface we want—the web, a native mobile app, plain text, or whatever else we can think of. If we look at it the right way, the GenServer for each game is really a microservice, or a nanoservice, living right inside the virtual machine.[1]

---

1. http://blog.plataformatec.com.br/2015/06/elixir-in-times-of-microservices/

Add a Web Interface with Phoenix

In Part 3, we'll generate a new Phoenix application without Ecto, the database layer that ships with Phoenix. We'll bring in our new Islands engine as a dependency and make it part of our new Phoenix application's supervision tree. We'll also see how to wire it up with the standard Phoenix MVC parts—the router, a controller, a view, and some templates.

Then we'll move on to the really exciting part: replacing HTTP's temporary client-server connections with persistent ones via Phoenix channels. Channels provide a conduit for lightning-fast message passing between front-end applications, and in our case, a stateful back-end server. We'll make good use of channel naming conventions to allow two players to connect to their own private GenServer running Islands. And we'll be able to run thousands of games simultaneously on a single server. Many languages would struggle to keep persistent connections open for all the players of all current games, but Elixir's incredible concurrency model will make it easy.

As we finish up, we'll have a web interface to our Islands engine. The main component will be a Phoenix channel able to connect two players directly to an individual Islands game. We'll customize the JavaScript files that Phoenix provides to get it primed and ready for your favorite front-end framework. When we're done, it'll have much less code and far fewer moving parts than a conventional web application.

Functional Web Development

With all this in mind, you may be wondering about the title of the book and how this represents *functional* web development.

One of the most characteristic patterns of functional programming is composition. With function composition, we take a big, complex piece of work and split it up into smaller, decoupled, and more focused functions. Then we re-create the full behavior by chaining these functions together. This not only helps us reason about our programs because smaller functions reduce cognitive load, but it helps with maintainability because smaller functions are easier to work on.

In this book, we'll take the idea of composition from the level of functions and scale it up to the level of applications. We'll take the full, complex behavior of a web application and separate it into independent, decoupled layers. Each layer will have a focused responsibility. It will do its job and nothing else.

Then we'll re-create the full behavior of the application by having each layer call into the next, passing the return values back up the chain and out to the client. By doing this, we'll gain clarity and maintainability for our whole application.

Now we're ready to introduce the game itself.

The Game of Islands

Let's talk a little bit about Islands. It's a game for two players, and each player has a board, which consists of a grid of one hundred coordinates. The grid is labeled with the numbers 1 through 10 across the top for the columns and down the left side for the rows. We name individual coordinates with this row-column combination.

The players cannot see each other's boards.

The players have matching sets of islands of various shapes and sizes, which they place on their own boards. The players can move the islands around as much as they like until they say that they are set. After that, the islands must stay where they are for the rest of the game.

Once both players have set their islands, they take turns guessing coordinates on their opponent's board, trying to find the islands. For every correct guess, we plant a palm tree on the island at that coordinate. When all the coordinates for an island have palm trees, the island is forested.

The first player to forest all of her opponent's islands is the winner.

Before we get to work, let's make sure we have all of our dependencies installed. For the first part of the book, all we'll need are Elixir and Erlang. For the second part, we'll need to install the Phoenix archive, Node.js, and npm. Have a look at the Appendix 1, *Installing System Dependencies*, on page 189 for help getting them installed.

We've got a plan! Time to start building.

Part I

Define the Functional Core in Elixir

In this first part, we will build all the logic for our game in a new Elixir project. We'll define the data and behavior that determines the essence of our application. We'll do this in sequential Elixir, with only modules and functions.

CHAPTER 2

Model Data and Behavior

There is a powerful opportunity at the very beginning of a new application. We've got ideas about what we want to build, but we haven't opened a terminal window or a text editor. The application is all potential, none of it yet actualized.

This is the perfect place to examine our habitual approaches and choose new paths. The decisions we make here will shape the rest of the project in fundamental ways.

The path we'll take is likely to be quite different from any you're used to, but it will simplify and clarify our code. It will build a foundation that the rest of the application can grow from.

As web developers, we typically begin a new project by running a command in our favorite framework to generate a new application we can customize. We also think about how to persist application state between requests. We define database schemas and write ORM models to do so.

We're going to turn that plan inside out. We'll begin by building the logic of the entire game in pure Elixir, using only data structures, functions, and modules. We won't touch a web framework until we introduce Phoenix in Part 3 of the book, and we won't use a database to store working application state.

We won't reach for OTP yet either. We'll bring it in as it becomes necessary, when we need concurrency and fault tolerance in Part 2.

The work we do in this chapter will define the most essential expression of any application written in a functional style—data and the functions that transform it. To get there, we'll create a new Elixir project. We'll take a good look at the application we're going to build and decide which data structures we'll need. Then we'll design functions to transform that data, creating the behavior we want.

Before we start writing code, let's think about what this approach will get us.

The Benefits

We're taking two radical steps with this approach, beginning an application without a framework, and choosing not to use a database for working state. We shouldn't make those decisions lightly. There should be some tangible benefits in return. By beginning this way, we gain focus, clarity, and simplicity.

Postpone Adding a Framework

Web frameworks are fantastic tools for developers. They give us real productivity gains by generalizing and automating the common, repetitive tasks of handling web requests.

Frameworks have their own domains, with their own entities—routes, controllers, models, views, and so on. These components are well suited for building web interfaces, but they make poor substitutes for business logic.

Our applications should have their own domains, completely separate from the framework. They should maintain a clean separation between the interface and the core application domain.

But building an application with a framework from the very beginning makes it nearly impossible to maintain that separation. This couples the interface and business logic, and makes it all too easy to begin thinking of framework components as part of the core application.

This has real consequences that we may not even notice. We'll cover these in detail in Chapter 6, *Generate a New Web Interface with Phoenix*, on page 131. By waiting to introduce Phoenix until we really need to expose our application to the web, we separate the concerns of our application from the concerns of its web interface. It frees us to focus on the pure domain of our application.

Postpone Adding Data Storage

Nobody can dispute the incredible utility databases provide. There's hardly an area of computing that isn't positively impacted by the ability to easily and quickly access data.

But when we begin an application knowing that we're going to use a database to store working application state, another distortion happens. We begin to think about our domain entities in database terms—foreign keys, join tables, even the idea of tables at all. We confuse the domain of the database with our own domain.

Then we typically go on to model our domain entities with ORMs as interfaces to the database. That makes us keep two representations of the domain entities in our heads: the ORM model and the database schema itself. This adds complexity and cognitive overhead.

In the end, we end up designing our application at least in part for the database instead of native code. We tend to forget that there are simpler and clearer ways to represent domain entities and the relationships between them.

We have wonderful tools right in front of us in the rich data structures that Elixir provides. By waiting to think about data persistence, we'll be able to work in a way that's natural for the application, not the database.

If the idea of avoiding a database completely is a nonstarter for you, hang tight. We'll talk about persistence for disaster recovery in Chapter 5, *Process Supervision for Recovery*, on page 97. We don't want anybody to lose any data!

Now that we've covered what we're doing and why we're doing it, it's time to get started.

Let's Build It

We'll begin by creating a brand-new Elixir application called islands_engine. We'll make it a supervised application, which most Elixir applications are, because process supervision is the mechanism that provides the tremendous fault tolerance we get from the BEAM. We'll look at supervisors in a lot more detail in Chapter 5, *Process Supervision for Recovery*, on page 97.

The command we'll use to create our new application is mix new islands_engine --sup:

```
$ mix new islands_engine --sup
* creating README.md
* creating .gitignore
* creating mix.exs
* creating config
* creating config/config.exs
* creating lib
* creating lib/islands_engine.ex
* creating lib/islands_engine/application.ex
* creating test
* creating test/test_helper.exs
* creating test/islands_engine_test.exs

Your Mix project was created successfully.
You can use "mix" to compile it, test it, and more:

    cd islands_engine
    mix test

Run "mix help" for more commands.
```

Let's take a look at what Mix generated for us:

```
$ cd islands_engine/
$ tree
.
├── README.md
├── config
│   └── config.exs
├── lib
│   ├── islands_engine
│   │   └── application.ex
│   └── islands_engine.ex
├── mix.exs
└── test
    ├── islands_engine_test.exs
    └── test_helper.exs

4 directories, 7 files
```

Mix created the skeleton of a standard Elixir/OTP application.

The mix new task created a directory for configuration, a directory for tests, and the lib/ directory for our code. The lib/islands_engine/application.ex file defines the application. Later, when we build in fault tolerance with a supervision tree, this is where we'll do it.

With a new project in place, it's time to get to work.

Discover the Entities and Model the Domain

This is the very first step in designing our application. We need to identify the entities of a system and represent them with the data structures we have available in Elixir.

To help us out, let's look at a picture of the game:

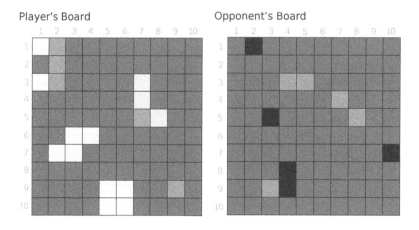

This shows what each of the players would see as they play. On the left is a view of their own board where players place their islands. The coordinates that make up the islands are the color of sand. When the player's opponent guesses correctly and hits an island, the coordinate the opponent hits will turn green. If all the coordinates that make up an island are hit, the island is forested, and when all of a player's islands are forested, the opponent has won the game.

On the right is a view of the opponent's board. This is where the player will guess coordinates by clicking on them. If a guess hits an island, that coordinate will turn green. Otherwise, it will turn black.

Just by describing that picture, we've identified four main entities: boards, islands, guesses, and coordinates.

From the image, we can see that there are two different kinds of boards with different representations. Each player's own board has islands as well as coordinates. The opponent's board has only coordinates.

The player's board has a set of islands, and each island is made up of a group of coordinates. The opponent's board is made up of three groups of coordinates: guessed coordinates that hit an island, guessed coordinates that missed all the islands, and all the unguessed coordinates.

We can also begin to think about this from another angle. As we talked about the image of the boards, we also talked about actions that can take place in the game. Any data structures we choose will need to support these actions as well:

- Players need to be able to position islands on their own boards.
- Players need to be able to guess coordinates on their opponent's boards.
- The game needs to determine if a guess results in a hit or a miss.
- The game needs to determine if a guess results in a forested island.
- The game needs to determine if a guess results in a win.

Now that we have some information to work with, let's start modeling the most common entity, coordinates.

Coordinate

Coordinates are ubiquitous in the game. They are the basic units of both players' boards and of islands as well.

We can identify individual coordinates by the combination of numbers for the row and the column. Passing around separate row and column values to represent a coordinate, though, is a little messy, and it doesn't capture the idea that those numbers represent a single entity. It would be better to combine them into a single data structure that we can pass around.

We have choices about how we could represent that. We might choose to use a tuple like this: {1, 1}. We should be careful about tuples if we're ever going to encode our data as JSON, which doesn't have a tuple type.

We might also choose a map, like this %{row: 1, col: 1}. It encapsulates both numbers into a single entity and is easy to pattern match against.

A third option is to use a struct. We'll be passing coordinates around to create islands and for players to guess. Structs maintain all the qualities of maps, but they offer compile-time checks on the keys, and they allow us to do run-time checks on the struct's type.

We'll be using coordinates and passing them around quite a bit, so the extra checks make structs seem like the way to go.

The first thing we'll need is a Coordinate module that aliases itself. Let's create that at lib/islands_engine/coordinate.ex:

```
defmodule IslandsEngine.Coordinate do
  alias __MODULE__
end
```

We can define a struct with row and col keys. Since we've aliased the Coordinate module, we can now refer to coordinate structs as %Coordinate{} instead of %IslandsEngine.Coordinate{}.

A coordinate needs both keys to have meaning. Neither a row nor a column by itself is very useful. Since we're using Elixir 1.4.0 or greater, we can include the @enforce_keys module attribute to ensure that both keys are present whenever we create a new struct:

```
model_data/lib/islands_engine/coordinate.ex
@enforce_keys [:row, :col]
defstruct [:row, :col]
```

Make sure that you define @enforce_keys before defstruct—otherwise it won't have any effect, and you'll get a warning saying that @enforce_keys was defined but never used.

We'll be using coordinate structs a lot, so it would be convenient to have a function that took in the row and column and gave us back a coordinate struct. We could create a new one by simply returning a struct with the correct values, like this:

```
def new(row, col), do:
  {:ok, %Coordinate{row: row, col: col}}
```

Since we have a single point where we're creating coordinate structs, we have an opportunity that we shouldn't miss. We saw in the image of the boards that both the rows and columns are numbered one through ten. This means that any values for row and col that are outside of that range are invalid.

We can use that range to validate the coordinate as we create it, returning an {:error, :invalid_coordinate} tuple if either value is outside the range:

```
model_data/lib/islands_engine/coordinate.ex
@board_range 1..10

def new(row, col)  when row in(@board_range) and col in(@board_range), do:
  {:ok, %Coordinate{row: row, col: col}}

def new(_row, _col), do: {:error, :invalid_coordinate}
```

Let's start up a new IEx session by running iex -S mix at the root of the project directory to see how this works:

```
$ iex -S mix
Erlang/OTP 19 [erts-8.2] [source] [64-bit] [smp:8:8] [async-threads:10]
             [hipe] [kernel-poll:false] [dtrace]

Compiling 2 files (.ex)
Interactive Elixir (1.4.2) - press Ctrl+C to exit (type h() ENTER for help)
```

Let's alias the module to save some typing:

```
iex> alias IslandsEngine.Coordinate
IslandsEngine.Coordinate
```

If we create a new coordinate with valid row and column values, we get a full coordinate struct back:

```
iex> Coordinate.new(1, 1)
{:ok, %IslandsEngine.Coordinate{col: 1, row: 1}}
```

If we give it values that are off the board, though, we get back an error:

```
iex> Coordinate.new(-1, 1)
{:error, :invalid_coordinate}
```

```
iex> Coordinate.new(11, 1)
{:error, :invalid_coordinate}
```

If we try to create a coordinate struct manually without both keys, we'll get an error:

```
iex> %Coordinate{row: 5}
** (ArgumentError) the following keys must also be given when building struct
    IslandsEngine.Coordinate: [:col]
    (new_islands) expanding struct: IslandsEngine.Coordinate.__struct__/1
                iex:4: (file)
```

With coordinates represented, let's move on to the less complex of the two boards: the opponent's board.

Guesses

The opponent's board is nothing but a group of guessed coordinates separated into those that hit an island and those that missed. There will be a large number of unguessed coordinates as well, but if we identify all the guesses, we can assume the rest are plain "ocean" coordinates.

This sounds like two lists: one list for hits and the other list for misses. We could wrap those lists in a struct with :hits and :misses keys, just as we did for coordinates.

There's something else to consider here, though. We can't necessarily guarantee that we'll receive any specific guess only once. Having unique lists of guessed coordinates would make it more efficient to re-create the opponent's board from scratch.

We could write our own functions to ensure uniqueness, but there's an easier way. We can use Elixir's MapSet data structure, which will guarantee that each member of the MapSet will be unique.

As we did with coordinates, let's create a new module for guesses at lib/islands_engine/guesses.ex. Following the pattern we set in the Coordinate module, we'll alias the Guesses module to reduce typing, enforce the :hits and :misses keys, and define the struct:

```
defmodule IslandsEngine.Guesses do
  alias __MODULE__

  @enforce_keys [:hits, :misses]
  defstruct [:hits, :misses]
end
```

Then we'll need a Guesses.new/0 function that returns a new guesses struct:

model_data/lib/islands_engine/guesses.ex
```
def new(), do:
  %Guesses{hits: MapSet.new(), misses: MapSet.new()}
```

Now let's start a new IEx session, alias the Coordinate and Guesses modules, and see how guesses work:

```
iex> alias IslandsEngine.{Coordinate, Guesses}
[IslandsEngine.Coordinate, IslandsEngine.Guesses]
```

Let's generate a new Guesses map and a few coordinates to experiment with:

```
iex> guesses = Guesses.new
%IslandsEngine.Guesses{hits: #MapSet<[]>, misses: #MapSet<[]>}

iex> {:ok, coordinate1} = Coordinate.new(1, 1)
{:ok, %IslandsEngine.Coordinate{col: 1, row: 1}}

iex> {:ok, coordinate2} = Coordinate.new(2, 2)
{:ok, %IslandsEngine.Coordinate{col: 2, row: 2}}
```

Now let's add coordinate1 to the set of hits with the Kernel.update_in/2 function. update_in/2 takes a path to the nested data structure we want to update and a function to transform its value. update_in/2 will pass that structure into the function as the first argument.

```
iex> guesses = update_in(guesses.hits, &MapSet.put(&1, coordinate1))
%IslandsEngine.Guesses{
  hits: #MapSet<[%IslandsEngine.Coordinate{col: 1, row: 1}]>,
  misses: #MapSet<[]>
}
```

There's the coordinate, in the hits set.

Note that what we did was just a transformation. The original value for guesses still exists. In order to hang on to the new value, we needed to rebind it to the guesses variable. Once that rebinding happens, the original value will fall out of scope and be garbage collected.

Now let's add coordinate2 to the :hits set as well:

```
iex> guesses = update_in(guesses.hits, &MapSet.put(&1, coordinate2))
%{hits: #MapSet<[
    %IslandsEngine.Coordinate{col: 1, row: 1},
    %IslandsEngine.Coordinate{col: 2, row: 2}
  ]>,
  misses: #MapSet<[]>}
```

That looks just the way we want it to.

Now let's try adding coordinate1 to the :hits set again:

```
iex> guesses = update_in(guesses.hits, &MapSet.put(&1, coordinate1))
%{hits: #MapSet<[
    %IslandsEngine.Coordinate{col: 1, row: 1},
    %IslandsEngine.Coordinate{col: 2, row: 2}
  ]>,
  misses: #MapSet<[]>}
```

That's great—coordinate1 still appears only once in the :hits set. It kept the set unique.

Let's move on to islands.

Islands

Islands are more complex than coordinates or guesses. They come in five different shapes: :atoll, :dot, :l_shape, :s_shape, and :square. Players can position them on the board, and their opponents try to guess their position.

Islands are made up of groups of coordinates. This suggests that we can use a list to represent them.

Looking back on our list of actions, one of the things we need to do is determine whether or not an island is forested—in other words, determine if all the coordinates of an island have been hit.

If we use a list to represent an island, we'll need to do two things. First, we'll need to mark coordinates as hit. Then, every time we need to see if the island is forested, we'll need to enumerate through the list.

Checking for a win would mean enumerating through all the coordinates in all the islands. The total number of coordinates is small, so it's not a really big deal, but we can do better.

If we saved two lists—one for the initial list of coordinates, and another to which we add any coordinates that are hit during a guess—we can do a simple comparison of the two lists.

There's a small problem with this, though. If we compare lists, the order of the elements matters.

```
iex> [1, 2] == [2, 1]
false
```

It's really unlikely that guesses will happen in the same order that the coordinates were added to an island, so that would force us to sort the lists each time we did a comparison or better yet, sort the initial coordinate list once, and subsequently sort only the list of hits every time we add a new one.

Fortunately, there's a really simple solution. If we use MapSet to store the two lists, order doesn't matter. We can use the built-in MapSet.equal?/2 function to determine equality:

```
iex> MapSet.equal?(MapSet.new([1, 2]), MapSet.new([2, 1]))
true
```

Just as we did with coordinates and guesses, we can wrap these two sets in a struct to package them as a single entity.

Now we're getting somewhere.

Let's create new Island module at lib/islands_engine/island.ex to capture what we've come up with so far:

```
defmodule IslandsEngine.Island do
  alias IslandsEngine.{Coordinate, Island}

  @enforce_keys [:coordinates, :hit_coordinates]
  defstruct [:coordinates, :hit_coordinates]

  def new(), do:
    %Island{coordinates: MapSet.new(), hit_coordinates: MapSet.new()}
end
```

We could keep the new/0 function as is, but there's something to consider. Each time a player places an island at a new position on the board, we'll need to pass it a full list of coordinates to store under the coordinates key. That's not a big problem, but if we leave the implementation as is, we would miss an opportunity.

It would be great if the new function could build all the coordinates for a full island automatically if we told it what type of island we wanted and gave it a coordinate to start from.

Let's solve that problem now.

We'll start with a :square island because it's a very regular shape that will make our technique easy to demonstrate. We'll also say that for all islands, we'll assume that the starting coordinate is in the upper-left corner.

With the starting coordinate set, we can think about what it would take to transform the row and column values of the starting coordinate in such a way that we generate all the other coordinates.

Here's how we could think about their relationships:

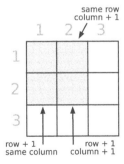

With that picture in mind, we can see the coordinates as a series of offsets from the starting coordinate:

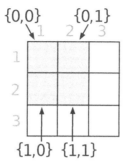

Let's experiment in the console to see how that might work.

Go ahead and alias the Coordinate module, and bind new row and col variables to 1, which represents the upper-left coordinate of the :square island:

```
iex> alias IslandsEngine.Coordinate
IslandsEngine.Coordinate

iex> row = 1
1

iex> col = 1
1
```

We can represent each of the offsets as a tuple, then pattern match on it to bind variables to the offset values:

```
iex> {row_offset, col_offset} = {0, 0}
{0, 0}
```

That gives us a way to build new coordinates based on their offsets from the original row and column values:

```
iex> Coordinate.new(row + row_offset, col + col_offset)
{:ok, %IslandsEngine.Coordinate{col: 1, row: 1}}
```

Fantastic. That's how we could build an actual %Coordinate{} for the upper-left part of a :square.

We could do the exact same thing for all the remaining coordinates represented by offset tuples, {0, 1}, {1, 0}, and {1, 1}. But constructing islands like this would be tedious and error prone. Let's create a list of offset tuples and automate the process with Enum.map/2:

```
iex> offsets = [{0, 0}, {0, 1}, {1, 0}, {1, 1}]
[{0, 0}, {0, 1}, {1, 0}, {1, 1}]
```

```
iex> Enum.map(offsets, fn {row_offset, col_offset} ->
...>   Coordinate.new(row + row_offset, col + col_offset)
...> end)
[ok: %IslandsEngine.Coordinate{col: 1, row: 1},
 ok: %IslandsEngine.Coordinate{col: 2, row: 1},
 ok: %IslandsEngine.Coordinate{col: 1, row: 2},
 ok: %IslandsEngine.Coordinate{col: 2, row: 2}]
```

Perfect. Now we can capture that list of offsets behind a private function that pattern matches for the type. We'll use this while creating an island in a minute.

```
defp offsets(:square),  do: [{0, 0}, {0, 1}, {1, 0}, {1, 1}]
```

That's the pattern we'll follow for the rest of the islands—determine the offsets we'll need to construct the island's coordinates and make them available with a private function.

Let's take a look at the atoll next.

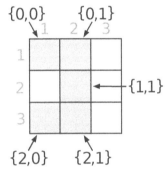

That gives us this list of offsets [{0, 0}, {0, 1}, {1, 1}, {2, 0}, {2, 1}] for the full island.

We'll add this to another clause of offsets/1:

```
defp offsets(:atoll),  do: [{0, 0}, {0, 1}, {1, 1}, {2, 0}, {2, 1}]
```

The dot island is the simplest:

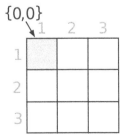

We simply use the row and col values for the starting coordinate itself:

```
defp offsets(:dot),     do: [{0, 0}]
```

On to the l-shaped island...

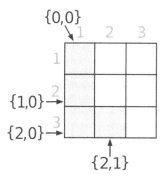

...which gives us this clause of offsets/1:

```
defp offsets(:l_shape), do: [{0, 0}, {1, 0}, {2, 0}, {2, 1}]
```

The s-shaped island is different because it doesn't actually use the starting coordinate in the island itself:

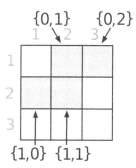

That gives us this clause of offsets/1:

```
defp offsets(:s_shape), do: [{0, 1}, {0, 2}, {1, 0}, {1, 1}]
```

In order to handle the case of an invalid island type, let's add one more clause to offsets/1 that matches anything and returns an error tuple:

```
defp offsets(_), do: {:error, :invalid_island_type}
```

Our plan will be to take the type, get the list of offsets for it with the private functions we defined, create coordinates with those offsets and the starting coordinate, populate a new MapSet with them, and finally assemble a complete island map.

Let's focus on creating all the coordinates for an island next. The idea is to enumerate over the list of offsets, create a new coordinate for each one, and put them all into the same set.

Enum.reduce/3 sounds like the right function to do that, but there's an issue here. It's quite possible that any of the offsets can create an invalid coordinate, one that's off the board.

Consider the case of a :square, which has an upper-left coordinate at row 10 and column 10. The offset {0, 1} would produce a new coordinate at row 10 and column 11, which is invalid.

This means we need to validate each coordinate as we build it and stop if we get an invalid one. Enum.reduce_while/3 is perfect for this. It takes an enumerable, a starting value for an accumulator, and a function to apply to each enumerated value. For us, those three arguments will be the list of offsets, a new MapSet, and a new function we'll get to in a minute.

The function we pass to Enum.reduce_while/3 must return one of two tagged tuples: either {:cont, some_value} to continue the enumeration, or {:halt, some_value} to end it.

We'll need a new function, add_coordinates/2, to wrap Enum.reduce_while/3 and return either the complete set of coordinates if all goes well, or an error tuple if we get an invalid coordinate. add_coordinates/2 will need to take both a list of offsets, and the upper-left coordinate so we know where to begin building the island coordinates from.

```
model_data/lib/islands_engine/island.ex
defp add_coordinates(offsets, upper_left) do
  Enum.reduce_while(offsets, MapSet.new(), fn offset, acc ->
    add_coordinate(acc, upper_left, offset)
  end)
end
```

Now we'll need to define that add_coordinate/3 function we just used in add_coordinates/2. It will take the set of coordinates we're building up, the upper-left coordinate, and the offset tuple.

```
model_data/lib/islands_engine/island.ex
defp add_coordinate(coordinates, %Coordinate{row: row, col: col},
    {row_offset, col_offset}) do
  case Coordinate.new(row + row_offset, col + col_offset) do
    {:ok, coordinate}               ->
      {:cont, MapSet.put(coordinates, coordinate)}
    {:error, :invalid_coordinate} ->
      {:halt, {:error, :invalid_coordinate}}
  end
end
```

Each time we build a new coordinate, we check to see if it is valid. If it is, we use MapSet.put/2 to add the new coordinate to the set and return it in the tagged :cont tuple. If the coordinate is invalid, we return {:halt, {:error, :invalid_coordinate}} to stop the enumeration. The error tuple will bubble up through add_coordinates/2 to the original caller.

Now it's time to delete the new/0 function we originally wrote, and put these pieces together in a new function to create an island.

The new/2 function will need an island type as well as the upper-left coordinate. We can do a runtime check of the upper-left coordinate by pattern matching for a %Coordinate{} struct.

The offsets/1 function we wrote earlier will check the island type. All valid types have a clause that returns a list of offset tuples, and the catchall clause will return an error.

```
def new(type, %Coordinate{} = upper_left) do
end
```

Within the body of new/2, there are two conditions we have to meet in order to produce a valid island. The offsets/1 function has to return a list of offsets instead of an invalid island key error, and add_coordinates/2 needs to return a MapSet instead of an invalid coordinate error. If both of those conditions pass, we can return a tagged tuple with :ok and the complete island.

In Elixir, the preferred way to handle multiple conditions like this is with the with/1 special form. This keeps all the validation in one place, and it gives us a single place to handle any errors that might come up.

```
model_data/lib/islands_engine/island.ex
def new(type, %Coordinate{} = upper_left) do
  with  [_|_] = offsets <- offsets(type),
        %MapSet{} = coordinates <- add_coordinates(offsets, upper_left)
  do
    {:ok, %Island{coordinates: coordinates, hit_coordinates: MapSet.new()}}
  else
    error -> error
  end
end
```

The else clause matches any error that might arise and passes it on. In practice, we're expecting this to be one of two types: either {:error, :invalid_island_type} if we've provided the wrong type, or {:error, :invalid_coordinate} if one of the offsets built an invalid coordinate.

Let's try this out in a new IEx session. We'll need to alias the Coordinate and Island modules:

```
iex> alias IslandsEngine.{Coordinate, Island}
[IslandsEngine.Coordinate, IslandsEngine.Island]
```

We'll try the successful case first by building an l-shaped island beginning at row 4 and column 6:

```
iex> {:ok, coordinate} = Coordinate.new(4, 6)
{:ok, %IslandsEngine.Coordinate{col: 6, row: 4}}

iex> Island.new(:l_shape, coordinate)
{:ok,
  %IslandsEngine.Island{
    coordinates: #MapSet<[
      %IslandsEngine.Coordinate{col: 6, row: 4},
      %IslandsEngine.Coordinate{col: 6, row: 5},
      %IslandsEngine.Coordinate{col: 6, row: 6},
      %IslandsEngine.Coordinate{col: 7, row: 6}
    ]>,
    hit_coordinates: #MapSet<[]>
  }
}
```

Nice! That worked.

Now let's try some things that should return an error, starting with passing in an invalid island key:

```
iex> Island.new(:wrong, coordinate)
{:error, :invalid_island_type}
```

That's perfect. Now let's use a valid type and coordinate, which happens to build an invalid coordinate as it applies the offsets:

```
iex> {:ok, coordinate} = Coordinate.new(10, 10)
{:ok, %IslandsEngine.Coordinate{col: 10, row: 10}}

iex> Island.new(:l_shape, coordinate)
{:error, :invalid_coordinate}
```

That's great—just what we want.

We've got one last entity to define: the player's board. Let's move on to that one now.

Boards

The player's board contains his islands, but it also brokers messages for them. Sometimes it will need to reference individual islands, like when it's checking to see if one is forested. Sometimes it will need to enumerate over all the islands—when it's checking for a win, for instance.

This points to representing them with a map, using island names as the keys. We can reference a given island with its key, ensure there are no duplicate island types, and enumerate over all the islands with any of the Enumerable functions.

Getting a new board is as simple as returning an empty map. We could do without this simple function, but it makes boards consistent with the rest of our domain entities.

Let's create a new Board module at lib/islands_engine/board.ex for this:

```
defmodule IslandsEngine.Board do
  def new(), do: %{}
end
```

That does it for data definition. Time to move on to more dynamic things.

Transforming Data

Applications need to actually do things to be useful. The essence of creating that behavior in functional programming is transforming data. This whole next section will be about just that—defining functions that transform the data structures we've defined.

Elixir gives us the pipeline operator |>, which allows us to elegantly take the output of a function and give it to another function as its first argument. It's tailor-made for the kind of work we'll be doing, and it's very idiomatic in Elixir.

We can think of pipelines as chaining functions together vertically. We can also chain them horizontally—functions calling functions either in the same module or across modules.

We'll use both approaches to take complex work, break it into smaller pieces, and compose the answer back together again.

Let's go through each of the modules we've defined so far, and write the functions we'll need to play the game.

Coordinates don't need to do anything more than they already do, so let's begin with guesses.

Guesses

As players guess coordinates in the game, we'll need to keep track of those guesses so that we can accurately represent their opponent's board. We'll never need to remove guessed coordinates—only add them.

We need a function to add guessed coordinates to a 'Guesses' struct, and determine whether they go into the set of hits or the set of misses. We'll create two function clauses for an 'add/3' function. Each clause will pattern match on whether the guess is a ':hit' or a ':miss' and put the coordinate in the appropriate set.

In order for this to work, we'll need to change the alias function slightly to include the Coordinate module:

```
alias IslandsEngine.{Coordinate, Guesses}
```

Now let's take a look at add/3:

```
model_data/lib/islands_engine/guesses.ex
def add(%Guesses{} = guesses, :hit, %Coordinate{} = coordinate), do:
  update_in(guesses.hits, &MapSet.put(&1, coordinate))

def add(%Guesses{} = guesses, :miss, %Coordinate{} = coordinate), do:
  update_in(guesses.misses, &MapSet.put(&1, coordinate))
```

We won't need an error clause here. In order to have determined whether a guessed coordinate was a hit or a miss, it must have gone through, and been validated by, another function. If the coordinate is no longer valid by this point, something is truly wrong and this function should cause a crash.

Let's see what this looks like in practice. Go ahead and start a new IEx session, and then alias IslandsEngine.Coordinate and IslandsEngine.Guesses:

```
iex> alias IslandsEngine.{Coordinate, Guesses}
[IslandsEngine.Coordinate, IslandsEngine.Guesses]
```

Now let's generate a new guesses map and add a few coordinates to it of both types:

```
iex> guesses = Guesses.new()
%IslandsEngine.Guesses{hits: #MapSet<[]>, misses: #MapSet<[]>}

iex> {:ok, coordinate1} = Coordinate.new(8, 3)
{:ok, %IslandsEngine.Coordinate{col: 3, row: 8}}

iex> guesses = Guesses.add(guesses, :hit, coordinate1)
%IslandsEngine.Guesses{
  hits: #MapSet<[%IslandsEngine.Coordinate{col: 3,
    row: 8}]>, misses: #MapSet<[]>
 }

iex> {:ok, coordinate2} = Coordinate.new(9, 7)
{:ok, %IslandsEngine.Coordinate{col: 7, row: 9}}

iex> guesses = Guesses.add(guesses, :hit, coordinate2)
%IslandsEngine.Guesses{
  hits: #MapSet<[
```

```
    %IslandsEngine.Coordinate{col: 3, row: 8},
    %IslandsEngine.Coordinate{col: 7, row: 9}
  ]>,
  misses: #MapSet<[]>
}

iex> {:ok, coordinate3} = Coordinate.new(1, 2)
{:ok, %IslandsEngine.Coordinate{col: 2, row: 1}}

iex> guesses = Guesses.add(guesses, :miss, coordinate3)
%IslandsEngine.Guesses{
  hits: #MapSet<[
    %IslandsEngine.Coordinate{col: 3, row: 8},
    %IslandsEngine.Coordinate{col: 7, row: 9}
  ]>,
  misses: #MapSet<[
    %IslandsEngine.Coordinate{col: 2, row: 1}
  ]>
}
```

That's exactly what we expected. Hit coordinates end up in the hits set and missed ones in the misses.

Islands have a little bit more to do during a game. Let's tackle islands next.

Island

An island has a role to play in three actions we've defined in the game: positioning islands, guessing coordinates, and checking for a forested island.

Since we've chosen MapSets to store coordinates and hit coordinates, we've got some powerful functions to help us out.

One thing we want to check for when positioning islands is that they don't overlap. We could rely solely on the front end to do this for us, but it's easy to check for and good to have backup validation on the back end.

We're representing islands as sets of coordinates. One way to determine if islands overlap is to look for any coordinates that they have in common. If there are any common coordinates between two islands, those islands overlap.

There's a great function to test for this: MapSet.disjoint?/2. Disjointed sets share no members, so if the coordinates of two islands are disjointed, they don't overlap.

model_data/lib/islands_engine/island.ex
```
def overlaps?(existing_island, new_island), do:
  not MapSet.disjoint?(existing_island.coordinates, new_island.coordinates)
```

We'll use this overlaps?/2 function later from a board to compare one island to all the existing ones.

Let's try this out in a new IEx session.

We'll need to generate a :square island as well as a :dot island that overlaps it. As a check, let's also generate an :l_shape island that doesn't overlap either of the other two.

```
iex> alias IslandsEngine.{Coordinate, Island}
[IslandsEngine.Coordinate, IslandsEngine.Island]

iex> {:ok, square_coordinate} = Coordinate.new(1, 1)
{:ok, %IslandsEngine.Coordinate{col: 1, row: 1}}

iex> {:ok, square} = Island.new(:square, square_coordinate)
{:ok,
  %IslandsEngine.Island{
    coordinates: #MapSet<[
      %IslandsEngine.Coordinate{col: 1, row: 1},
      %IslandsEngine.Coordinate{col: 1, row: 2},
      %IslandsEngine.Coordinate{col: 2, row: 1},
      %IslandsEngine.Coordinate{col: 2, row: 2}
    ]>,
    hit_coordinates: #MapSet<[]>
  }
}

iex> {:ok, dot_coordinate} = Coordinate.new(1, 2)
{:ok, %IslandsEngine.Coordinate{col: 2, row: 1}}

iex> {:ok, dot} = Island.new(:dot, dot_coordinate)
{:ok,
  %IslandsEngine.Island{
    coordinates: #MapSet<[
      %IslandsEngine.Coordinate{col: 2, row: 1}
    ]>,
    hit_coordinates: #MapSet<[]>
  }
}

iex> {:ok, l_shape_coordinate} = Coordinate.new(5, 5)
{:ok, %IslandsEngine.Coordinate{col: 5, row: 5}}

iex> {:ok, l_shape} = Island.new(:l_shape, l_shape_coordinate)
{:ok,
  %IslandsEngine.Island{
    coordinates: #MapSet<[
      %IslandsEngine.Coordinate{col: 5, row: 5},
      %IslandsEngine.Coordinate{col: 5, row: 6},
      %IslandsEngine.Coordinate{col: 5, row: 7},
      %IslandsEngine.Coordinate{col: 6, row: 7}
    ]>,
    hit_coordinates: #MapSet<[]>
  }
}
```

With those islands created, we can use them to see overlaps?/2 in action:

```
iex> Island.overlaps?(square, dot)
true

iex> Island.overlaps?(square, l_shape)
false

iex> Island.overlaps?(dot, l_shape)
false
```

Perfect. That's exactly the right result.

Let's turn our attention to guessing a coordinate. We'll need a guess/2 function to do that. It will take an island and a coordinate.

If a guessed coordinate is a member of the coordinates set, we need to transform the island by adding the coordinate to the hit coordinates set, and then return a tuple containing :hit and the transformed island.

If the guessed coordinate isn't in the coordinates set, we don't need to do any transformation, and we can just return :miss.

The MapSet module provides a member?/2 function that tests whether something is a member of a given set. That will make this check easy.

```
model_data/lib/islands_engine/island.ex
def guess(island, coordinate) do
  case MapSet.member?(island.coordinates, coordinate) do
    true ->
      hit_coordinates = MapSet.put(island.hit_coordinates, coordinate)
      {:hit, %{island | hit_coordinates: hit_coordinates}}
    false -> :miss
  end
end
```

The board will use this function as it tests all islands for a guessed coordinate.

Now that we have guessing covered, let's work on checking whether an island is forested. We just need to return a Boolean, so we won't actually transform any data. Here again, a MapSet function comes in handy. We can make this a one-liner by comparing the equality of an island's coordinates and hit coordinates. If they are equal, the island is forested; otherwise it isn't.

```
model_data/lib/islands_engine/island.ex
def forested?(island), do:
  MapSet.equal?(island.coordinates, island.hit_coordinates)
```

We're ready to try out these two functions in the IEx session we had going a moment ago.

First, let's recompile the Island module so that we'll have access to the guess/2 and forested?/1 functions we just wrote:

```
iex> r Island
warning: redefining module IslandsEngine.Island (current version defined in memory)
  lib/islands_engine/island.ex:1

{:reloaded, IslandsEngine.Island, [IslandsEngine.Island]}
```

The r/1 Function

 The IEx helper function r/1 recompiles a single module and loads the newly recompiled code into memory. It won't touch the .beam file for that module on disk.

This is different from another IEx helper function, recompile/0. recompile/0 recompiles the whole project from IEx instead of a single module.

Then let's create a new dot island. It'll take one successful guess to forest it.

```
iex> {:ok, dot_coordinate} = Coordinate.new(4, 4)
{:ok, %IslandsEngine.Coordinate{col: 4, row: 4}}

iex> {:ok, dot} = Island.new(:dot, dot_coordinate)
{:ok,
 %IslandsEngine.Island{
   coordinates: #MapSet<[
     %IslandsEngine.Coordinate{col: 4,row: 4}
   ]>,
   hit_coordinates: #MapSet<[]>}
}
```

If we guess an incorrect coordinate, we should get only :miss in return. Since there was no data transformation, the island itself should remain exactly as it was.

```
iex> {:ok, coordinate} = Coordinate.new(2, 2)
{:ok, %IslandsEngine.Coordinate{col: 2, row: 2}}

iex> :miss = Island.guess(dot, coordinate)
:miss

iex> dot
%IslandsEngine.Island{
  coordinates: #MapSet<[
    %IslandsEngine.Coordinate{col: 4, row: 4}
  ]>,
  hit_coordinates: #MapSet<[]>}
```

Perfect—that's exactly what we expected.

Now let's guess the correct coordinate. That should do two things: add the coordinate to the hit coordinates set, and return {:hit, island} with the transformed island.

```
iex> {:ok, new_coordinate} = Coordinate.new(4, 4)
{:ok, %IslandsEngine.Coordinate{col: 4, row: 4}}

iex> {:hit, dot} = Island.guess(dot, new_coordinate)
{:hit,
 %IslandsEngine.Island{
   coordinates: #MapSet<[%IslandsEngine.Coordinate{col: 4, row: 4}]>,
   hit_coordinates: #MapSet<[%IslandsEngine.Coordinate{col: 4, row: 4}]>}
 }
```

That makes the coordinates and the hit coordinates sets equal, so now forested?/1 should return true.

```
iex> Island.forested?(dot)
true
```

That's perfect. There's one last function we'll need—just a small one that returns the list of valid island types. The board will need this to check whether the board has positioned all the valid types.

model_data/lib/islands_engine/island.ex
```
def types(), do: [:atoll, :dot, :l_shape, :s_shape, :square]
```

That covers all the functionality we'll need for islands. Let's move on to the last module: Board.

Board

The board has a dual role to play. It knows about and can address all the islands. It can delegate function calls down to them individually or as a group. That makes a board both an orchestrator as well as an interface for actions that involve islands.

The actions that a board needs to handle include positioning islands, ensuring that all islands are positioned, and guessing coordinates. Let's tackle them in order.

Players will be able to move their islands around the board until they declare them set. Each time they move them, the front end of the application will pass down an atom key representing the type of the island, as well as the row and column of the starting coordinate.

Layers above this one will convert those to an actual island as well as passing both the key and the island into the board here. As long as the island matches an %Island{}, we know it's valid. If it doesn't match, this will raise a

FunctionClauseError. That's appropriate because it means something went really wrong with the island after it was created.

In order to shorten that runtime check on an %Island{} struct, let's add an alias at the top of the module file:

```
alias IslandsEngine.Island
```

If the island doesn't overlap any existing islands, we set it in the board map with the key we passed in. Otherwise, we return {:error, :overlapping_island}.

model_data/lib/islands_engine/board.ex
```
def position_island(board, key, %Island{} = island) do
  case overlaps_existing_island?(board, key, island) do
    true  -> {:error, :overlapping_island}
    false -> Map.put(board, key, island)
  end
end
```

The private function overlaps_existing_island?/3 lets us know if there is any overlap. It does this by enumerating over the islands to see if there are any for which Island.overlaps?/2 returns true.

It also does a quick check to make sure we're only checking the islands that we aren't replacing. We don't care about the one we are replacing because it's going away.

model_data/lib/islands_engine/board.ex
```
defp overlaps_existing_island?(board, new_key, new_island) do
  Enum.any?(board, fn {key, island} ->
    key != new_key and Island.overlaps?(island, new_island)
  end)
end
```

In the course of the game, players can move their islands around as often as they want until they declare them set. After both players declare their islands set, it will be the first player's turn to guess.

We want to make sure that a player has positioned an island for all the island types before declaring his islands set, and that's what all_islands_positioned?/1 does. It gets the list of valid island types from the Island.types/0 function.

model_data/lib/islands_engine/board.ex
```
def all_islands_positioned?(board), do:
  Enum.all?(Island.types, &(Map.has_key?(board, &1)))
```

Now let's move on to guessing coordinates. We'll need a guess/2 function that takes a board map and a coordinate, and checks the board to see if that coordinate matches any in an island.

The goal of the guess/2 function is to reply with four pieces of information: whether the guess was a hit or a miss, either :none or the type of island that was forested, :win or :no_win, and finally the board map itself.

We've ensured that no island will overlap any other. That means that every coordinate in an island is unique. No other island will have that coordinate. Because of that, each guess could match at most one coordinate.

We'll do a runtime check to make sure we get a valid coordinate struct, so let's add the Coordinate module to our aliases:

```
alias IslandsEngine.{Coordinate, Island}
```

The sequence we'll follow is to check all the islands in the board for a match and then formulate the full response. That sounds like a great fit for a pipeline.

```
model_data/lib/islands_engine/board.ex
def guess(board, %Coordinate{} = coordinate) do
  board
  |> check_all_islands(coordinate)
  |> guess_response(board)
end
```

We don't yet have the 'check_all_islands/2' or 'guess_response/2' functions. Let's fix that next.

Board.check_all_islands/2 will need a board so it will have access to that board's islands, and it will need a coordinate to check for. With those, we can use Enum.find_value/3 to do the checking.

Enum.find_value/3 works like Enum.find/3. Both functions take an enumerable, a default value, and a function to apply on each enumeration. Both will halt the enumeration once the function returns a truthy value.

The main difference is that find/3 returns the element for the enumeration, and find_value/3 sends back the return value of the function.

We'll set the default return to be :miss. That's what check_all_islands/3 will return if Enum.find_value/3 doesn't get a truthy value.

```
model_data/lib/islands_engine/board.ex
defp check_all_islands(board, coordinate) do
  Enum.find_value(board, :miss, fn {key, island} ->
    case Island.guess(island, coordinate) do
      {:hit, island} -> {key, island}
      :miss          -> false
    end
  end)
end
```

If the guess does result in a hit, we'll need to return both the island key and the island itself. When a guess hits a coordinate, we store that coordinate in the island. That means we'll need to replace the new island value in the board using the key. We'll also need to check whether or not that island was forested.

Now let's tackle the last piece we'll need for guesses: the response.

If the guess is a miss, we know that it could not have forested an island, and it could not have won the game. That makes the response easy.

If the guess was a hit, we need to check whether the guess forested the island and whether it won the game.

model_data/lib/islands_engine/board.ex
```
defp guess_response({key, island}, board) do
  board = %{board | key => island}
  {:hit, forest_check(board, key), win_check(board), board}
end
defp guess_response(:miss, board), do: {:miss, :none, :no_win, board}
```

In guess_response/2, we reference forest_check/2 and win_check/1 that we don't currently have. Let's take care of those next.

Let's look at the forested part of the response first. The Island.forested?/2 function only returns a Boolean, not the island type. We'll need two extra functions in this chain to get that data. Board.forest_check/2 calls into Board.forested?/2, which is a pass through to the Island function of the same name. If Island.forested?/2 returns true, so will Board.forested/2, and that will trigger Board.forest_check/2 to return the type. Otherwise, it will return :none.

model_data/lib/islands_engine/board.ex
```
defp forest_check(board, key) do
  case forested?(board, key) do
    true  -> key
    false -> :none
  end
end

defp forested?(board, key) do
  board
  |> Map.fetch!(key)
  |> Island.forested?()
end
```

In the course of a guess, the board will also need to determine whether or not the guess resulted in a win. This will require a function chain as well. Checking for a win means checking to see if all the islands on that board are forested. We'll need to check in with Island.forested?/1 for each island on the board. The function that does that is Board. all_forested?/1.

The return value we need will be either :win or :no_win. Board.all_forested?/1 returns a Boolean, so we'll need another function to translate that Boolean into one of the two possible responses. If Board.all_forested?/1 returns true, we return :win. Otherwise, we return :no_win.

```
model_data/lib/islands_engine/board.ex
defp win_check(board) do
  case all_forested?(board) do
    true  -> :win
    false -> :no_win
  end
end

defp all_forested?(board), do:
  Enum.all?(board, fn {_key, island} -> Island.forested?(island) end)
```

Now we're ready to take the code we've written so far out for a spin in IEx.

Putting the Pieces Together

A player's own board acts as an interface. It's the front door to the data and functions that make up the game. Now that we've completely defined the Board module, we're ready to see how all of the work we've done so far fits together.

Let's start a new session with iex -S mix, and alias the Board, Coordinate, and Island modules:

```
iex> alias IslandsEngine.{Board, Coordinate, Island}
[IslandsEngine.Board, IslandsEngine.Coordinate, IslandsEngine.Island]
```

Then we can generate a new board:

```
iex> board = Board.new()
%{}
```

Now let's generate a new square island and position it on the board:

```
iex> {:ok, square_coordinate} = Coordinate.new(1, 1)
{:ok, %IslandsEngine.Coordinate{col: 1, row: 1}}

iex> {:ok, square} = Island.new(:square, square_coordinate)
{:ok,
  %IslandsEngine.Island{
    coordinates: #MapSet<[
      %IslandsEngine.Coordinate{col: 1, row: 1},
      %IslandsEngine.Coordinate{col: 1, row: 2},
      %IslandsEngine.Coordinate{col: 2, row: 1},
      %IslandsEngine.Coordinate{col: 2, row: 2}
    ]>,
    hit_coordinates: #MapSet<[]>
  }
}
```

```
iex> board = Board.position_island(board, :square, square)
%{square: %IslandsEngine.Island{
    coordinates: #MapSet<[
      %IslandsEngine.Coordinate{col: 1, row: 1},
      %IslandsEngine.Coordinate{col: 1, row: 2},
      %IslandsEngine.Coordinate{col: 2, row: 1},
      %IslandsEngine.Coordinate{col: 2, row: 2}
    ]>,
  hit_coordinates: #MapSet<[]>}
}
```

As a test, let's create a new dot island that overlaps the square and try to position it on the board:

```
iex> {:ok, dot_coordinate} = Coordinate.new(2, 2)
{:ok, %IslandsEngine.Coordinate{col: 2, row: 2}}
```

```
iex> {:ok, dot} = Island.new(:dot, dot_coordinate)
{:ok,
  %IslandsEngine.Island{
    coordinates: #MapSet<[%IslandsEngine.Coordinate{col: 2, row: 2}]>,
    hit_coordinates: #MapSet<[]>
  }
}
```

```
iex> Board.position_island(board, :dot, dot)
{:error, :overlapping_island}
```

We get an error, which is exactly what we would expect. Note that we didn't rebind the board variable, so it has remained unchanged. Now let's generate a new dot island that doesn't overlap the square, and position it on the board:

```
iex> {:ok, new_dot_coordinate} = Coordinate.new(3, 3)
{:ok, %IslandsEngine.Coordinate{col: 3, row: 3}}
```

```
iex> {:ok, dot} = Island.new(:dot, new_dot_coordinate)
{:ok,
  %IslandsEngine.Island{
    coordinates: #MapSet<[
      %IslandsEngine.Coordinate{col: 3, row: 3}
    ]>,
    hit_coordinates: #MapSet<[]>
  }
}
```

```
iex> board = Board.position_island(board, :dot, dot)
%{dot: %IslandsEngine.Island{
    coordinates: #MapSet<[
      %IslandsEngine.Coordinate{col: 3, row: 3}
    ]>,
    hit_coordinates: #MapSet<[]>
  },
```

```
    square: %IslandsEngine.Island{
      coordinates: #MapSet<[
        %IslandsEngine.Coordinate{col: 1, row: 1},
        %IslandsEngine.Coordinate{col: 1, row: 2},
        %IslandsEngine.Coordinate{col: 2, row: 1},
        %IslandsEngine.Coordinate{col: 2, row: 2}
    ]>,
    hit_coordinates: #MapSet<[]>
    }
}
```

Great—we're able to position it on the board the way we want. Now we can try a guess. Let's try for a miss first. We should get back a four tuple that looks like {:miss, :none, :no_win, board}.

```
iex> {:ok, guess_coordinate} = Coordinate.new(10, 10)
{:ok, %IslandsEngine.Coordinate{col: 10, row: 10}}
```

```
iex> {:miss, :none, :no_win, board} = Board.guess(board, guess_coordinate)
{:miss, :none, :no_win,
 %{dot: %IslandsEngine.Island{
        coordinates: #MapSet<[
          %IslandsEngine.Coordinate{col: 3, row: 3}
        ]>,
        hit_coordinates: #MapSet<[]>
      },
   square: %IslandsEngine.Island{
     coordinates: #MapSet<[
       %IslandsEngine.Coordinate{col: 1, row: 1},
       %IslandsEngine.Coordinate{col: 1, row: 2},
       %IslandsEngine.Coordinate{col: 2, row: 1},
       %IslandsEngine.Coordinate{col: 2, row: 2}
     ]>,
     hit_coordinates: #MapSet<[]>}
   }
 }
```

That's exactly what we do get back. Now let's try for a guess that doesn't forest an island or win. We can guess one of the coordinates in the square. That should also give us back a four tuple, but this time it'll look like {:hit, :none, :no_win, board}.

```
iex> {:ok, hit_coordinate} = Coordinate.new(1, 1)
{:ok, %IslandsEngine.Coordinate{col: 1, row: 1}}
iex> {:hit, :none, :no_win, board} = Board.guess(board, hit_coordinate)
{:hit, :none, :no_win,
 %{dot: %IslandsEngine.Island{
     coordinates: #MapSet<[%IslandsEngine.Coordinate{col: 3, row: 3}]>,
     hit_coordinates: #MapSet<[]>},
   square: %IslandsEngine.Island{
     coordinates: #MapSet<[
       %IslandsEngine.Coordinate{col: 1,row: 1},
```

```
    %IslandsEngine.Coordinate{col: 1, row: 2},
    %IslandsEngine.Coordinate{col: 2, row: 1},
    %IslandsEngine.Coordinate{col: 2, row: 2}
  ]>,
 hit_coordinates: #MapSet<[%IslandsEngine.Coordinate{col: 1, row: 1}]>}}}
```

Again that's just what we expected.

Next we'll try for a win. Instead of tediously guessing the rest of the coordinates, we'll cheat a little. We can make the square's hit coordinates equal to its coordinates. That will automatically make it a forested island, and it will leave the single coordinate of the dot island as the only unguessed coordinate.

```
iex> square = %{square | hit_coordinates: square.coordinates}
%IslandsEngine.Island{
  coordinates: #MapSet<[
    %IslandsEngine.Coordinate{col: 1, row: 1},
    %IslandsEngine.Coordinate{col: 1, row: 2},
    %IslandsEngine.Coordinate{col: 2, row: 1},
    %IslandsEngine.Coordinate{col: 2, row: 2}
  ]>,
 hit_coordinates: #MapSet<[
   %IslandsEngine.Coordinate{col: 1, row: 1},
   %IslandsEngine.Coordinate{col: 1, row: 2},
   %IslandsEngine.Coordinate{col: 2, row: 1},
   %IslandsEngine.Coordinate{col: 2, row: 2}
 ]>}
```

We'll need to reposition the square after we manipulate it:

```
iex> board = Board.position_island(board, :square, square)
%{dot: %IslandsEngine.Island{
    coordinates: #MapSet<[
      %IslandsEngine.Coordinate{col: 3, row: 3}
    ]>,
   hit_coordinates: #MapSet<[]>},
  square: %IslandsEngine.Island{
    coordinates: #MapSet<[
      %IslandsEngine.Coordinate{col: 1, row: 1},
      %IslandsEngine.Coordinate{col: 1, row: 2},
      %IslandsEngine.Coordinate{col: 2, row: 1},
      %IslandsEngine.Coordinate{col: 2, row: 2}
    ]>,
   hit_coordinates: #MapSet<[
     %IslandsEngine.Coordinate{col: 1, row: 1},
     %IslandsEngine.Coordinate{col: 1, row: 2},
     %IslandsEngine.Coordinate{col: 2, row: 1},
     %IslandsEngine.Coordinate{col: 2, row: 2}
   ]>
  }
}
```

Now when we guess the dot coordinate, we should get a :hit, the :dot island should be forested, and we should get a :win.

```
iex> {:ok, win_coordinate} = Coordinate.new(3, 3)
{:ok, %IslandsEngine.Coordinate{col: 3, row: 3}}

iex> {:hit, :dot, :win, board} = Board.guess(board, win_coordinate)
{:hit, :dot, :win,
 %{dot: %IslandsEngine.Island{
     coordinates: #MapSet<[
       %IslandsEngine.Coordinate{col: 3, row: 3}
     ]>,
     hit_coordinates: #MapSet<[
       %IslandsEngine.Coordinate{col: 3, row: 3}
     ]>},
   square: %IslandsEngine.Island{
     coordinates: #MapSet<[
       %IslandsEngine.Coordinate{col: 1, row: 1},
       %IslandsEngine.Coordinate{col: 1, row: 2},
       %IslandsEngine.Coordinate{col: 2, row: 1},
       %IslandsEngine.Coordinate{col: 2, row: 2}
     ]>,
     hit_coordinates: #MapSet<[
       %IslandsEngine.Coordinate{col: 1, row: 1},
       %IslandsEngine.Coordinate{col: 1, row: 2},
       %IslandsEngine.Coordinate{col: 2, row: 1},
       %IslandsEngine.Coordinate{col: 2, row: 2}
     ]>
   }
 }
}
```

Fantastic—that's exactly what we do get.

With that, we've defined all the behavior we need from the entities we've defined.

Wrapping Up

We've made good progress so far. We modeled the most important building blocks of the game. We can see how coordinates compose into islands and boards.

Our domain is simpler because of the approach we've taken. Our domain entities live single lives in our application instead of double lives in both the application and the database. Application behavior comes from simple functions that transform data. There's not an ORM in sight.

While we are in a good position, the code we currently have allows any action to happen at any time. There's no sense of sequence to the events. There's nothing to prevent us from guessing coordinates before we position any islands.

Before the code we now have can become a real game, we'll need to define and enforce the order in which events can happen. That's what our task will be for the next chapter.

What we'll do in this chapter
- *get an overview of how state machines work*
- *model application rules as states and transitions*
- *build a state machine to embody the rules*

CHAPTER 3

Manage State with a State Machine

Handling state is an important topic in web development these days. We're seeing changing ideas and practices in both the front- and back-end worlds. It's time we talk more directly about how to manage state in an Elixir project.

The BEAM's concurrency and fault tolerance bring truly stateful web applications within reach. But stateful applications bring their own challenges. Managing state over time requires great care and coordination. Keeping code clean in the process provides an extra level of difficulty.

We'll meet these challenges with a purely functional state machine. We'll see how to use a data structure and multiple clauses of a single function to make decisions and enforce rules in an application.

Our state machine will help us coordinate events and transitions as well. Most importantly, we'll keep our code clean by separating state management from business logic.

Our first step will be to think a little bit about what state really means.

A Quick Look at State

Holding state is an act of remembering. What we're remembering is the data that models our system. We especially care about the transformation of that data resulting from actions taken in the system over time. The way we remember is to commit the data to memory on the host machine.

The reason we save state is so future actions can be consistent with the past. Say we created a new user profile in an application. If the user wants to change his email address later on, we better still have access to his original profile.

Most web applications present a twist to this story. As we mentioned in Chapter 1, *Mapping Our Route*, on page 1, HTTP is a stateless protocol. It is specifically designed not to remember anything about requests—actions in the system—as soon as they are fulfilled.

As web developers, we typically get around this by storing state in a database. Since we're not using a database, we need another place to store state data over time. In Islands, we'll store it in long-running Elixir processes, specifically GenServer processes.

In Chapter 2, *Model Data and Behavior*, on page 9, we developed the data to model the domain for Islands. We also wrote functions to transform that data. This is where we currently stand; we have data, but it is not yet state.

In Chapter 4, *Wrap It Up in a GenServer*, on page 65, we'll see how to hold that data and its subsequent transformations in GenServer processes. This act of holding data in a process over time will transform the data structures we now have into state.

Before we move on to where we're going, though, let's see where we've been.

A Bit of History

Early client-server applications were stateful. Clients connected to the server and stayed connected while they passed messages back and forth. Think mainframe applications with dedicated terminals as clients.

That worked well, but it meant that the number of possible clients was limited by system resources like memory, CPU, and the number of concurrent processes the system could support.

The web gets around these limitations because of the nature of HTTP. When a client makes an HTTP request to a server, it must supply all the data the server will need to fulfill that request. Once the server sends its response, it forgets everything it just knew about both the request and the client.

This request-response cycle has been critical to the success and scaling of the web. It requires fewer system resources to handle vastly more requests because the server doesn't need to keep track of anything once it sends a response. This allows applications to use less expensive shared pools for resources like database or mainframe connections instead of more expensive dedicated resources for each client. Applications can manage other resources like threads and memory the same way.

HTTP shed resource costs, but it picked up others along the way. It's impractical to pass all the state a complex application needs to do its work. Instead, servers store that state in a database, and clients pass along only enough information for the server to fetch that data to fulfill the request. If the request involves any change in state, the server needs to write those changes back to the database. These trips to and from the database add latency. Modeling a domain for a database adds unnecessary complexity.

As developers, we pick up the tab for these added costs in terms of extra code to write and maintain as well as extra cognitive load when reasoning about our applications.

Change Is Afoot

As applications grow and traffic increases, these costs begin to really add up. At serious scale, they can become prohibitive, so people are looking for ways to get around them.

We're at the beginning of a sea change in web development. We're seeing the return of stateful servers with persistent client connections. Modern hardware provides abundant system resources. Elixir provides more than enough power and concurrency to handle application state and persistent connections at scale. Phoenix channels make writing those persistent connections a breeze.

With stateful applications, we no longer have the luxury of clean state with every new request. We have to manage state over time, and make sure it remains consistent. We need to understand the stages an application can go through, and handle the transitions between them. We need to ensure that events in the system are consistent with the stage the application is in.

The Front-end World

Front-end JavaScript developers have already walked this path from a mostly stateless to a stateful environment. With the rise of Ajax requests a number of years ago, front-end web applications could fetch data outside of the normal request-response cycle. They could update the DOM without a full page reload that would wipe the state clean.

The rise of Ajax opened up incredible possibilities in user interactions. Web applications became as complex and interesting as desktop apps—map applications, email, and office suites. With the vastly increased time between page reloads, the browser suddenly became a stateful environment, and developers quickly found that they needed strategies to manage state.

The JavaScript world is still grappling with this shift. The community is continually inventing new solutions to ease the difficulty of handling state—frameworks, data binding libraries, promise libraries, generators, and more. The sheer number of solutions out there and the speed with which they hit the ecosystem creates a very real sense of fatigue.

A Different Path

You might think that we could make decisions about application stages, stage transitions, and events with conditional logic. You would be right, but the costs would be high. The number of nested "if" statements necessary to do the job would lead to a snarl of code paths. Real readability and maintainability problems would be our reward.

We're going to choose a different direction. We'll implement our own purely functional state machine to handle all the stages that Islands will go through in the course of a full game. It's going to make decisions for the application about which actions to allow and which to deny at a given stage. It will manage transitions from one stage to the next, and it will help the game enforce the rules.

By implementing our own state machine, we'll keep the logic for managing state separate from the rest of the game logic. This separation of concerns will keep our code clean, readable, and maintainable.

Before we go any further, let's get a better understanding of state machines in general and take a look at an example of a problem that's ideal for a state machine to solve.

State Machines

State machines are fundamental to computation. A finite state machine is a form of abstract machine. It defines a finite number of states a system can be in, as well as any events in the system that can trigger transitions between those states. Any time we need to model a complex process that proceeds through a number of states, especially ones that might loop back to earlier states, we should think about reaching for a finite state machine.

The Meaning of "State"

We need to resolve an ambiguity with the word "state." In Elixir, when we say "state," we mean data held in an Elixir process. In a state machine, a "state" is the name of a stage an application can go through. In this chapter, we'll use "state" to mean the name of a stage in an application.

Let's walk through an example of a problem that's perfect for a state machine. Imagine you're working at an e-commerce site with its own warehouse. As part of your job, you need to model and control the life cycle of a product from the first time a buyer sees it at a trade show until it's stocked in the warehouse and available for sale.

There are a surprising number of states a product can go through. If a buyer sees a product they like and adds it to the system, that first state could be called scouted. After that, a buyer might order a sample. We could call that state sample_ordered. Once the sample arrives, the buyer might accept it and order a larger number of them. We might call that state inventory_ordered. The buyer might also reject the sample and have the state go back to scouted.

There are rules here, and a sense of progression. Buyers can't order a sample unless they've scouted the product. They can't order inventory until they've ordered a sample, and so on.

This process might continue until the buyer accepts the production run, the warehouse completes the intake of the merchandise, and the warehouse has stocked the product in preparation for fulfillment. It might also stop at any point and go back to a previous state if something goes wrong.

This scenario demonstrates the transitions between states, but it glosses over a really important component. There are events in the system that trigger the state transitions. Buyers add products to the system. That's an event. Buyers order samples. Shipments arrive. Buyers accept samples, and so on. All events.

These are the keys to understanding state machines. Events trigger state transitions. The state machine may progress to a new state or regress to a previous one depending on the event and the current state.

That's all great information, but now we need to translate it into executable code for our game.

A Functional State Machine for Islands

Many language ecosystems provide ready-made state machine packages that we can customize to fit our own applications. Elixir is no exception to this in that OTP has a fine state machine called :gen_statem built in.

We could use :gen_statem to implement our state machine, but we're going to build our own from scratch instead. We'll be able to do it in much fewer lines of code, and we won't need to spin up a new process for each state machine the way we would if we used :gen_statem.

Instead, we'll define a new module, multiple clauses of a single function, and a data structure to represent the state. Each time we invoke the function, we'll pass in the state as well as an event. The function will decide whether or not to permit that combination of state and event. It will also decide whether or not to transition to a new state.

If we return a tuple tagged with :ok, that means the combination is permissible. By returning :error, we signify that it is not. In effect, we'll be creating a whitelist of permissible state/event combinations.

This may all seem a little abstract at the moment. Hang in there. It'll become clear as we go along. Let's get started!

Defining the Rules

We're about to see just how flexible a data structure and a single function can be. We could use this same pattern to create state machines that fit the needs of any application we're working on.

Before we write any code, it's helpful to have a picture of what we need to build, what the pieces look like, and how they fit together. Here's a representation of the state machine we need to implement, including all the states and the direction of the transitions between them.

We're going to build our state machine one state at a time in the order the states follow as the game progresses. For each state, we'll add to the whitelist of allowable event/state combinations and trigger state transitions where they are needed. The place to begin is with a new module and function. That's where we'll go next.

Start with a Catchall Clause

Our goal is to build a whitelist, but we still need to account for all the error cases that won't match it. That's the job of a catchall clause, and that's what we'll define in this section.

Let's start with a new file at lib/islands_engine/rules.ex. We'll need to define the IslandsEngine.Rules module in it and alias it as well:

```
defmodule IslandsEngine.Rules do
  alias __MODULE__
end
```

We'll need to address the basic question of how to represent the state in the system. We can start with a struct that has a :state key. The initial state for Islands is :initialized, so we can set the state key to that when we define the struct:

```
defstruct state: :initialized
```

With this representation, transitioning state means transforming the value of the :state key for this struct.

As we've done with all the modules we've defined so far, let's define a function that returns a new data structure that represents this module:

state_machine/lib/islands_engine/rules.ex
```
def new(), do: %Rules{}
```

The one function we'll need for all the whitelist definition work will be check/2. The catchall clause for it will take a state and an action. Then it will just return :error. We won't pattern match on any specific values, so this clause will always match.

state_machine/lib/islands_engine/rules.ex
```
def check(_state, _action), do: :error
```

Clause Order Matters

Since this catchall clause will always match, it's important to define it after all the other clauses of check/2. Otherwise, it will prevent any other `check/2` clauses defined after it from ever matching.

For any state/event combination that ends up in this catchall, we don't want to transition the state. By simply returning :error, we don't transform the value of the :state key. Leaving it unchanged keeps the game in the same state.

Working Through the States

With the catchall in place, all we need to do from now on is define the positive cases. We'll add a new clause of check/2 for each new state/event pair that we want to add to the whitelist. By the end of this section, we will have a complete state machine that will describe all the rules of Islands.

Let's start with the first state, :initialized.

Initialized

When we're in :initialized, the only permissible action is adding the second player. We're going to focus on that one action and the transition it triggers, from :initialized to :players_set.

We'll need a clause of check/2 for this that adds this combination of state and event to the whitelist.

The idea that we want to express is that when we're in the :initialized state, it's okay to add a new player, and when that action happens, we should transition the state to :players_set.

This clause of check/2 will need to pattern match for a state of :initialized as well as the action :add_player. Then we'll return a two tuple tagged with :ok. In order to represent the state change, the second element of that return tuple will be a transformed %Rules{} struct with a new state value, :players_set.

Just by returning that new value for the state key, we'll have a new state. We won't need to configure all the possible states beforehand.

state_machine/lib/islands_engine/rules.ex
```
def check(%Rules{state: :initialized} = rules, :add_player), do:
  {:ok, %Rules{rules | state: :players_set}}
```

We're doing a runtime check on the %Rules{} struct to make sure that's what we're getting, and then we pattern match on the state from there.

It's important to mention that this function doesn't actually add another player. It makes a decision about whether it's okay to add another player based on the current state of the game. That's all there is to it. Let's give it a try in IEx:

```
iex> alias IslandsEngine.Rules
IslandsEngine.Rules

iex> rules = Rules.new()
%IslandsEngine.Rules{state: :initialized}

iex> {:ok, rules} = Rules.check(rules, :add_player)
{:ok, %IslandsEngine.Rules{state: :players_set}}

iex> rules.state
:players_set
```

That's exactly what we want. Calling the check/2 function with :add_player when we're in the :initialized state returns {:ok, <new rules>} and moves us into the :players_set state.

Adding a player is the only event we allow in the :initialized state. We need to return an error for any other event associated with that state. The catchall clause we've already defined should already handle this. Let's try it out:

```
iex> rules = Rules.new()
%IslandsEngine.Rules{state: :initialized}

iex> :error = Rules.check(rules, :completely_wrong_action)
:error

iex> rules.state
:initialized
```

That's just what we were looking for. With that, we're ready to move on to the next state.

Players Set

At this point, the second player has joined the game so we are in the :players_set state. In :players_set, the players can position and reposition their islands on the board without transitioning the state.

They can also set their islands, declaring their positions fixed for the rest of the game. When only one player has set her islands, the game remains in :players_set. When the second player sets his islands, the game transitions to the :player1_turn state. That's when the game really begins.

Those are the events and the transition we'll focus on here, from :players_set to :player1_turn.

Let's begin by defining a clause of check/2 for players positioning their islands.

The idea that we would like to express with this clause is that when the game is in :players_set, it's okay for either of the players to position their islands.

```
def check(%Rules{state: :players_set} = rules, {:position_islands, player}) do
  {:ok, rules}
end
```

That definition seems fine, but there's a subtlety here that we need to capture.

Players can move their islands at any time until they set them. Both players are almost certain to set their islands at different times. If player1 has set her islands but player2 hasn't, player1 should no longer be able to move her islands, but player2 should still be able to. While this condition exists, the state machine should remain in the :players_set state.

In other words, when in the :players_set state, the state machine can have two different conditions:

- neither player has set his islands
- one player has set her islands and the other hasn't

The second player setting his islands is the event that triggers a state change.

To handle this properly, we need to keep track of whether each of the players have set their islands individually. We need to save this data in the state machine, and the rules struct is the right place to do it. Let's add to the struct definition at the top of the Rules module. The new keys will be :player1 and :player2. The default values will be :islands_not_set.

state_machine/lib/islands_engine/rules.ex
```
defstruct state: :initialized,
          player1: :islands_not_set,
          player2: :islands_not_set
```

Now we can use the data in the rules struct to make the right decisions. We get the player in the tuple representing the action. With that and a case statement, we can craft a response.

state_machine/lib/islands_engine/rules.ex
```
def check(%Rules{state: :players_set} = rules, {:position_islands, player}) do
  case Map.fetch!(rules, player) do
    :islands_set -> :error
    :islands_not_set -> {:ok, rules}
  end
end
```

If the value for the player key is :islands_not_set, it's fine for that player to move her islands, so we return {:ok, rules}. If the values is :islands_set, it's not okay for her to move her islands, so we return :error. Neither action is enough to transition the state out of :players_set, so we leave the rules struct alone.

Let's check this in a new console session. We'll need a new rules struct with the state set to :players_set.

If you've still got the session running from the last section, remember to recompile the Rules module with the r/1 function. Otherwise, alias IslandsEngine.Rules.

```
iex> r Rules
warning: redefining module IslandsEngine.Rules (current version loaded
  from _build/dev/lib/new_islands/ebin/Elixir.IslandsEngine.Rules.beam)
  lib/new_islands/rules.ex:1

{:reloaded, IslandsEngine.Rules, [IslandsEngine.Rules]}

iex> rules = Rules.new()
%IslandsEngine.Rules{player1: :islands_not_set, player2: :islands_not_set,
 state: :initialized}

iex> rules = %{rules | state: :players_set}
%IslandsEngine.Rules{player1: :islands_not_set, player2: :islands_not_set,
 state: :players_set}

iex> rules.state
:players_set
```

Great! Now let's try out this new clause:

```
iex> {:ok, rules} = Rules.check(rules, {:position_islands, :player1})
{:ok,
 %IslandsEngine.Rules{player1: :islands_not_set, player2: :islands_not_set,
   state: :players_set}}

iex> {:ok, rules} = Rules.check(rules, {:position_islands, :player2})
{:ok,
 %IslandsEngine.Rules{player1: :islands_not_set, player2: :islands_not_set,
   state: :players_set}}

iex> rules.state
:players_set
```

Perfect! That's what we want.

We still need to handle players setting their islands. Let's define a new clause for that next.

We should always let a player set his islands, but we only transition the state when both players have their islands set.

We can handle the first part, changing the value of the player key, with this:

```
def check(%Rules{state: :players_set} = rules, {:set_islands, player}) do
  rules = Map.put(rules, player, :islands_set)
end
```

Now we need to handle the second part. The question is whether check/2 should transition the state machine to :player1_turn. That should happen only if both players have set their islands. We can check for that with a private function:

```
state_machine/lib/islands_engine/rules.ex
defp both_players_islands_set?(rules), do:
  rules.player1 == :islands_set && rules.player2 == :islands_set
```

If both_players_islands_set?/1 returns true, then we should transition to :player1_turn. Otherwise, we should just return {:ok, <current rules>}.

```
state_machine/lib/islands_engine/rules.ex
def check(%Rules{state: :players_set} = rules, {:set_islands, player}) do
  rules = Map.put(rules, player, :islands_set)
  case both_players_islands_set?(rules) do
    true  -> {:ok, %Rules{rules | state: :player1_turn}}
    false -> {:ok, rules}
  end
end
```

Let's see how this works in the console. We'll get a new rules struct and set its state to :players_set.

Again, either recompile or alias IslandsEngine.Rules.

```
iex> rules = Rules.new()
%IslandsEngine.Rules{player1: :islands_not_set, player2: :islands_not_set,
  state: :initialized}
```

```
iex> rules = %{rules | state: :players_set}
%IslandsEngine.Rules{player1: :islands_not_set, player2: :islands_not_set,
  state: :players_set}
```

Let's have :player1 set her islands. There should be nothing stopping her from doing this multiple times, but if only :player1 has set her islands, the state should remain :players_set.

```
iex> {:ok, rules} = Rules.check(rules, {:set_islands, :player1})
{:ok,
 %IslandsEngine.Rules{player1: :islands_set, player2: :islands_not_set,
  state: :players_set}}
```

```
iex> {:ok, rules} = Rules.check(rules, {:set_islands, :player1})
{:ok,
  %IslandsEngine.Rules{player1: :islands_set, player2: :islands_not_set,
  state: :players_set}}
```

```
iex> rules.state
:players_set
```

That's exactly what we see.

Since :player1 just set her islands, she shouldn't be able to position them any more, but :player2 still should be able to:

```
iex> Rules.check(rules, {:position_islands, :player1})
:error
```

```
iex> {:ok, rules} = Rules.check(rules, {:position_islands, :player2})
{:ok,
 %IslandsEngine.Rules{player1: :islands_set, player2: :islands_not_set,
  state: :players_set}}
```

Perfect. That's what we want.

Now let's have :player2 set his islands and do the same check. After we do this, both players will have set their islands, so the state should transition to :player1_turn:

```
iex> {:ok, rules} = Rules.check(rules, {:set_islands, :player2})
{:ok,
 %IslandsEngine.Rules{player1: :islands_set, player2: :islands_set,
  state: :player1_turn}}
```

```
iex> Rules.check(rules, {:position_islands, :player2})
:error
```

```
iex> rules.state
:player1_turn
```

We said that a player can set his islands as many times as he wants when the game is in :players_set. Let's see if :player2 can set her islands again:

```
iex> Rules.check(rules, {:set_islands, :player2})
:error
```

Apparently, she can't.

The reason :player2 can't set her islands a second time is that the state is now :player1_turn and we haven't defined any permissible actions for that state yet.

Now that we're in a state that we haven't created any whitelisted actions for, we shouldn't be able to do anything:

```
iex> rules.state
:player1_turn

iex> Rules.check(rules, :add_player)
:error

iex> Rules.check(rules, {:position_islands, :player1})
:error

iex> Rules.check(rules, {:position_islands, :player2})
:error

iex> Rules.check(rules, {:set_islands, :player1})
:error
```

This behaves exactly as we want it to. Time to tackle the next state.

Player One's Turn

Not all state transitions are one-way. State machines often need to revisit previous states based on events in the system. Taking turns in a game is a perfect example of this. In a two-person game, the state will transition back and forth between one player's turn and the other until one of them wins.

We're at the point where both players have set their islands, and the game is in :player1_turn. When it's the first player's turn, that player may guess a coordinate, and that player may win the game. No other events are permissible.

When :player1 guesses a coordinate, the state should transition to :player2_turn. And if :player1 wins, the state should transition to :game_over. We'll focus on the transition from :player1_turn to :player2_turn first.

We'll need a new clause of check/2 for this. What we want to express with this clause is that when it is player1's turn, it is okay for player1 to guess a coordinate, and the state should transition to :player2_turn.

This new clause will need to pattern match for the state :player1_turn and a tuple representing the idea that :player1 wants to guess a coordinate.

state_machine/lib/islands_engine/rules.ex
```
def check(%Rules{state: :player1_turn} = rules, {:guess_coordinate, :player1}), do:
  {:ok, %Rules{rules | state: :player2_turn}}
```

That should do it. Let's take it out for a spin in a new IEx session to make sure. Let's get a new rules struct, and set the state to :player1_turn:

```
iex> rules = Rules.new()
%IslandsEngine.Rules{player1: :islands_not_set, player2: :islands_not_set,
 state: :initialized}

iex> rules = %{rules | state: :player1_turn}
%IslandsEngine.Rules{player1: :islands_not_set, player2: :islands_not_set,
 state: :player1_turn}

iex> rules.state
:player1_turn
```

We should get an error if :player2 tries to guess a coordinate:

```
iex> Rules.check(rules, {:guess_coordinate, :player2})
:error
```

So far, so good. It should be okay for :player1 to guess a coordinate, and that should transition the state to :player2_turn.

```
iex> {:ok, rules} = Rules.check(rules, {:guess_coordinate, :player1})
{:ok,
 %IslandsEngine.Rules{player1: :islands_not_set, player2: :islands_not_set,
  state: :player2_turn}}

iex> rules.state
:player2_turn
```

Fabulous. That worked just as we expected. The game alternates between :player1_turn and :player2_turn until one player wins. When a player does win, the game transitions to the :game_over state.

We'll need a new clause of check/2 that describes winning when the game is in :player1_turn.

When we defined the Board.guess/2 function, we made sure part of its return tuple specified whether the guess resulted in a win or not with :win or :no_win.

We can use those values in two new clauses of check/2 to determine whether or not the state machine should transition to :game_over. If it does transition, we'll need to transform the rules struct to reflect that transition before we return it.

```elixir
state_machine/lib/islands_engine/rules.ex
def check(%Rules{state: :player1_turn} = rules, {:win_check, win_or_not}) do
  case win_or_not do
    :no_win -> {:ok, rules}
    :win -> {:ok, %Rules{rules | state: :game_over}}
  end
end
```

Let's try it out in IEx. If you're continuing with the same session, remember to recompile the Rules module; otherwise, alias it.

We'll need a new rules struct set to :player1_turn:

```elixir
iex> rules = Rules.new()
%IslandsEngine.Rules{player1: :islands_not_set, player2: :islands_not_set,
 state: :initialized}

iex> rules = %{rules | state: :player1_turn}
%IslandsEngine.Rules{player1: :islands_not_set, player2: :islands_not_set,
 state: :player1_turn}
```

Then we can test out the :no_win clause of check/2:

```elixir
iex> {:ok, rules} = Rules.check(rules, {:win_check, :no_win})
{:ok,
 %IslandsEngine.Rules{player1: :islands_not_set, player2: :islands_not_set,
  state: :player1_turn}}

iex> rules.state
:player1_turn
```

Perfect—that left us in the :player1_turn state. Now let's try the :win clause:

```elixir
iex> {:ok, rules} = Rules.check(rules, {:win_check, :win})
{:ok,
 %IslandsEngine.Rules{player1: :islands_not_set, player2: :islands_not_set,
  state: :game_over}}

iex> rules.state
:game_over
```

It works! Now let's build the transition back to :player1_turn.

Player Two's Turn

This state is the mirror image of :player1_turn. When it's the second player's turn, he can guess a coordinate or win the game. No other events are permissible. Much of this will seem familiar as we'll need the same two clauses we defined for :player1_turn and :player1, but this time for :player2_turn and :player2.

The first clause should say that when the state is :player2_turn, :player2 is allowed to guess, and that guess will transition the state to :player1_turn:

state_machine/lib/islands_engine/rules.ex
```
def check(%Rules{state: :player2_turn} = rules, {:guess_coordinate, :player2}), do:
  {:ok, %Rules{rules | state: :player1_turn}}
```

The other two states should say that if a guess didn't result in a win, we don't transition the state, but if it did result in a win, we should transition to :game_over.

state_machine/lib/islands_engine/rules.ex
```
def check(%Rules{state: :player2_turn} = rules, {:win_check, win_or_not}) do
  case win_or_not do
    :no_win -> {:ok, rules}
    :win -> {:ok, %Rules{rules | state: :game_over}}
  end
end
```

Now that we have these function clauses defined, let's move on to the last state of the game.

Game Over

State machines often, but not always, have an end state, one from which we can't transition. In Islands, we do have an end state: :game_over.

We won't need any new clauses of check/2 for the :game_over state because there are no new actions to add to the whitelist. The catchall clause will return an error no matter what we try to do when the state is :game_over.

At this point we can see our state machine make it through all the states, trying all the events. Let's start a new IEx session, get a new rules struct, and make sure it's in the :initialized state:

```
iex> alias IslandsEngine.Rules
IslandsEngine.Rules

iex> rules = Rules.new()
%IslandsEngine.Rules{player1: :islands_not_set, player2: :islands_not_set,
 state: :initialized}

iex> rules.state
:initialized
```

Then we can check on adding a player and make sure that we transition to
:players_set:

```
iex> {:ok, rules} = Rules.check(rules, :add_player)
{:ok,
 %IslandsEngine.Rules{player1: :islands_not_set, player2: :islands_not_set,
  state: :players_set}}
```

```
iex> rules.state
:players_set
```

Each player should be able to move an island and the state should still be
:players_set:

```
iex> {:ok, rules} = Rules.check(rules, {:position_islands, :player1})
{:ok,
 %IslandsEngine.Rules{player1: :islands_not_set, player2: :islands_not_set,
  state: :players_set}}
```

```
iex> rules.state
:players_set
```

```
iex> {:ok, rules} = Rules.check(rules, {:position_islands, :player2})
{:ok,
 %IslandsEngine.Rules{player1: :islands_not_set, player2: :islands_not_set,
  state: :players_set}}
```

```
iex> rules.state
:players_set
```

When one player sets her islands, she should no longer be able to position
them, but the other player still should be able to:

```
iex> {:ok, rules} = Rules.check(rules, {:set_islands, :player1})
{:ok,
 %IslandsEngine.Rules{player1: :islands_set, player2: :islands_not_set,
  state: :players_set}}
```

```
iex> rules.state
:players_set
```

```
iex> Rules.check(rules, {:position_islands, :player1})
:error
```

```
iex> {:ok, rules} =  Rules.check(rules, {:position_islands, :player2})
{:ok,
 %IslandsEngine.Rules{player1: :islands_set, player2: :islands_not_set,
  state: :players_set}}
```

```
iex> rules.state
:players_set
```

When both players set their islands, the state should transition to :player1_turn:

```
iex> {:ok, rules} = Rules.check(rules, {:set_islands, :player2})
{:ok,
 %IslandsEngine.Rules{player1: :islands_set, player2: :islands_set,
   state: :player1_turn}}
```

```
iex> rules.state
:player1_turn
```

Now the players should be able to alternate guessing coordinates, beginning with :player1. If :player2 tries to guess first, that should be an error. After that, the players will alternate guesses.

```
iex> Rules.check(rules, {:guess_coordinate, :player2})
:error
```

```
iex> {:ok, rules} = Rules.check(rules, {:guess_coordinate, :player1})
{:ok,
 %IslandsEngine.Rules{player1: :islands_set, player2: :islands_set,
   state: :player2_turn}}
```

```
iex> rules.state
:player2_turn
```

```
iex> Rules.check(rules, {:guess_coordinate, :player1})
:error
```

```
iex> {:ok, rules} = Rules.check(rules, {:guess_coordinate, :player2})
{:ok,
 %IslandsEngine.Rules{player1: :islands_set, player2: :islands_set,
   state: :player1_turn}}
```

```
iex> rules.state
:player1_turn
```

Any guess that doesn't result in a win should not transition the state. But when somebody does win, the state should become :game_over:

```
iex> {:ok, rules} = Rules.check(rules, {:win_check, :no_win})
{:ok,
 %IslandsEngine.Rules{player1: :islands_set, player2: :islands_set,
   state: :player1_turn}}
```

```
iex> rules.state
:player1_turn
```

```
iex> {:ok, rules} = Rules.check(rules, {:win_check, :win})
{:ok,
 %IslandsEngine.Rules{player1: :islands_set, player2: :islands_set,
   state: :game_over}}
```

```
iex> rules.state
:game_over
```

That all looks fantastic.

This brings us to the end of the game. We've defined all the function clauses of check/2 that represent the permissible events in each state of the game. We've got a catchall clause to handle any combination not on the whitelist.

But we've actually done more than that. We've created a simple system, separate from the business logic, that can help manage complex, long-running processes. We can use the ideas we've covered in this chapter anywhere we need to make decisions about application state.

Now the application logic needs to make use of it. That's coming up next.

Wrapping Up

We've done a lot of great work in this chapter. We've built a state machine from scratch, encapsulating all the rules of Islands with a data structure and a handful of clauses for a single function.

Along the way, you learned a lot about finite state machines in general. You saw how to map events to states in order to make decisions about behavior. You learned how to manage state and state transitions.

The implementation we came up with is completely decoupled from any of the other modules we've written so far. It can decide whether actions follow the rules independently, without any knowledge of the application logic for the rest of the game.

Now we're ready to put all the work we've done so far together in a single entity, with a single interface. As we move into Part 2 of the book, we'll define a GenServer for the game. In it, we'll get the application logic working together with the rules.

By the end of the next chapter, Islands is really going to take shape. It's going to feel a lot more like a complete game. Let's get to it!

Part II

Add OTP for Concurrency and Fault Tolerance

With the logical core of our application complete, it's time to step into the world of concurrency and parallelism. OTP will guide our way as we build a GenServer for concurrency and add a supervisor for fault tolerance and recovery.

What we'll do in this chapter

- *implement a GenServer for the game logic*
- *define a public interface for the game server process*
- *practice common patterns in OTP Behaviours*
- *initialize GenServers with the correct state*
- *use process registration to name individual games*

CHAPTER 4

Wrap It Up in a GenServer

We're about to make a big leap. Up to this point, we've focused on modules, functions, and data. This is the synchronous side of Elixir, the world within a process where code executes sequentially. In this chapter, we'll be moving into the asynchronous side, the world of processes and message passing that provides Elixir's world-class concurrency and parallelism.

We're going to build a GenServer that contains all the data and game logic for Islands. We'll spin up new instances of this GenServer as separate processes, one for each individual game. By the time it's complete, all the work we've done so far will come together in a single entity with a unified interface.

This move is important on its own, but on a deeper level, it points to something even more significant. We'll see the ways in which GenServers provide much of what we want from micro-services while solving many of the problems micro-services can cause.

Here's the plan. We'll define a new module and turn it into a GenServer. We'll see how to spawn new processes with it, and have those processes hold game data as their state. As we customize its behavior, we'll define public functions that will act as the interface to the game. In Part 3, as we layer on Phoenix, we'll use these functions as a way of interacting with each game process.

Before we execute that plan, let's take a closer look at micro-services, and the problems they're intended to solve as well as the problems they create. Then we'll see how OTP addresses the problems without creating new ones.

A Look at Micro-Services

Let's face it—applications just naturally grow, and often they grow too large and complex to easily manage. The impulse to break large applications up into smaller, independent ones has been around a long time. Micro-services are currently the most popular approach for this, but long before micro-services, there was SOA, service-oriented architecture.

Breaking up large applications is a scaled-up version of the impulse we have to break up larger functions into smaller ones with intention-revealing names, and then compose those functions back together to re-create the original behavior. We get the bigger picture from the recomposition, and we can dig into the details by looking at the individual functions.

The key to that recomposition for services is communication. Since they are separate, services need an external mechanism to talk to each other. Most often, that is an HTTP request from one service to another, but it can also be a message queue like RabbitMQ or a streaming log like Kafka.

This separation—and need for communication—is exactly the source of all the benefits as well as all the problems associated with breaking an application up into services. Let's take a closer look at both sides of the micro-services coin.

The Advantages

The forces that push developers to reach for services are direct and easy to enumerate: the need for focus, encapsulation, and scale.

Unix taught us the virtue of doing one thing and doing it well. Code that is smaller and more focused is easier to write and maintain. Unix also taught us that we can compose smaller commands together to build more complex behavior. These same ideas scale up to services.

Well-designed services hide all their data and implementation details behind a public interface. This allows us to change the implementation behind the scenes as much as we need to as long as we preserve the contract of the interface.

Different parts of a monolithic application often have very different resource needs. By breaking applications up into services, we can address those needs individually, on a service-by-service basis.

The Pain Points

The benefits services provide come at a cost, and that cost can be high. Development, testing, and deployment all become more complex. Handling failure when a service crashes or loses communication over the network takes extra thought, preparation, and work.

Development and testing pose similar problems. When services depend on one another for the full application to work, either we need to start all the services up for the system to work, or we need to provide mock services in their stead.

If we choose to use live services, we need to make sure we keep the versions up to date. If we choose mock services, we need to make sure they haven't drifted and that they still accurately represent the real service.

Deployment is vulnerable to the versioning problem as well. Managing version changes across multiple services requires careful planning. Handling breaking changes to one service means that we'll need to update others that depend on it. That often leads to multiple deployments at once to keep the whole system consistent.

We also need a new strategy for cross-service fault tolerance—how we keep other services up and running well when one of the services is down or unavailable. One way of doing this is with a circuit breaker pattern.

Circuit breakers monitor external calls for failure or timeouts. They keep the whole system from failing by providing predetermined responses instead of crashing. They may also implement retry strategies to determine when a failed service comes back.

One of the biggest pain points of all is determining where to break a monolith apart. As an industry, we don't yet have a well-defined language of patterns we can rely on to make these decisions the way we do for object-oriented (OO) design and refactoring.

When we do OO design or refactoring, we have language-level structures appropriate for the job—classes, methods, modules, and functions. But when we're breaking a monolith into services, most languages don't have constructs at the scale needed to hold a service.

Other languages and ecosystems offer solutions to these problems, but the solutions often add complexity and friction to our workflow. In the Erlang and Elixir ecosystems, OTP provides solutions without the extra overhead.

Let's take a look at what OTP has to offer.

OTP Solutions

OTP is Erlang's extended standard library. It includes a number of software tools and a set of design patterns. Together, these are a treasure trove of collected wisdom and best practices for building concurrent and fault-tolerant programs in Elixir and Erlang.

OTP stands for Open Telecom Platform. The name reflects Erlang's origin in the telecom industry at Ericsson. In practice, OTP is much more general than the name suggests. We can build any type of application with OTP.

OTP's toolset is extensive. It includes an in-memory key-value store (ETS), a relational database (Mnesia), monitoring and debugging tools (Observer, Debugger), a release management tool (Reltool), a static analysis tool (Dialyzer)—and that list just begins to scratch the surface. We won't cover these here, but it's good to know that they are there if you need them.

One of the most common and powerful tools OTP provides are the design patterns called Behaviours. Two Behaviours in particular give us much of what we want from micro-services without the problems—GenServer and Application.

We'll take a look at those in just a minute, but first let's see what Behaviours are all about.

Behaviours

For the next few chapters, we're going to see a lot of OTP *Behaviours*. Coming up with a concise explanation of what OTP Behaviours are is difficult. In concrete terms, they are modules in OTP as well as modules that we define in our Elixir applications. But they are also design patterns that reflect best practices. The rest of this section should clear things up.

Behaviours grew out of the experience of early Erlang developers at Ericsson. Concurrency is hard. Fault tolerance is hard. The Erlang team put a lot of work into getting them right. Behaviours standardize their best practices and make them easy to use in our own applications.

OTP defines Behaviours for different types of specialized processes that we can use to build our own applications. We've already mentioned GenServer and Application, but there are others. There's one for finite state machines, one for creating and handling system events, and one for creating supervisors for fault tolerance. We can also define our own custom Behaviours to work in our own domains if we need to.

Each Behaviour is a module in OTP that contains the common code necessary for a process of that type. A GenServer, for instance, needs to be able to start new server processes, hold state, handle synchronous calls with a return value, as well as handle asynchronous casts without a return. The Behaviour module defines all that wiring and plumbing.

For real applications, the wiring and plumbing are not enough. We need to be able to customize a GenServer to handle the very specific requests our applications require.

Fortunately, there's an easy way to do this. We start by defining a normal module in our application. Then we inject the Behaviour module code into our new module. A Behaviour stores a list of callbacks—specific to it—that modules like ours need to implement in order to be an instance of that Behaviour. By writing those callbacks with code specific to our application, we customize our implementation of the Behaviour to work exactly the way we need it to.

That's the process we'll follow to build a GenServer for Islands.

GenServer

GenServer is an Elixir Behaviour that wraps its Erlang counterpart, :gen_server. GenServer automatically creates default implementations of the :gen_server callbacks so that we only write code specific to our GenServer. We'll use the Elixir GenServer as we build our game server, which will spare us from writing a lot of boilerplate.

GenServer processes provide most of what we want from services, and they address the problems that services create as well. They are separate Elixir processes that listen for and respond to messages from other processes. They can hold state as well as take action in the system.

Because they are separate processes that share nothing with other processes, we get the isolation and encapsulation that we're looking for. We can spawn new processes to address scaling needs, and do it at a very granular level.

Elixir applications that use GenServer processes are just normal Elixir applications. There's no extra work necessary to set up a development environment. We won't need any external means to allow a GenServer process to communicate with the rest of the application.

Testing works exactly the same as with any other Elixir app. There's no need to mock another service because the application remains a single whole.

Deployments are the same as well. Whatever deployment strategy you currently use will just work. Since the GenServer is integrated with the rest of the application, there's no way to create a version mismatch.

We don't need extra planning or work to ensure fault tolerance. GenServer processes can be supervised, so we naturally get a level of fault tolerance that's very difficult to match in any other system.

Application

Elixir Application Behaviours take on the "where to divide a monolith into services" question. They are that intermediary organizing construct that most languages lack.

Like GenServer, Application is an Elixir Behaviour that wraps its OTP counterpart, :application. Application provides default implementations for :application callbacks.

The first thing we need to clear up is the name. An Application is not what we usually think of as a complete software application. It's closer to what we would call a library or a package in other ecosystems. They are a little different, though. Applications are supervised units of code that start and stop as a single entity.

We can use them as libraries or packages if we want, but they can also be integral, named, delineated parts of an application. They naturally define facets we can break an application apart by if our needs demand it.

Back when we generated our islands_engine project in Chapter 2, *Model Data and Behavior*, on page 9, we noted that Elixir had generated it as an Application for us. That's good news because we've been working with an Application all along without any extra effort on our part.

We'll see how using an Application makes separating game logic from the web interface easy in Chapter 6, *Generate a New Web Interface with Phoenix*, on page 131. We'll also see that Applications have a role to play in process supervision in Chapter 5, *Process Supervision for Recovery*, on page 97.

Now it's time to write some code.

Getting Started with GenServer

GenServers are everywhere in Elixir code. Becoming proficient with GenServer is one of the best things you can do to level up as an Elixir developer. It will require some work on your part. You'll need to learn how client functions, module functions, and callbacks work and interact.

But honestly, implementing a GenServer is pretty straightforward. We'll get lots of practice in this chapter, so you'll come out of it knowing your way around.

Let's begin with a new file in the lib directory called lib/islands_engine/game.ex. This will define a new module that will become our GenServer.

```elixir
defmodule IslandsEngine.Game do
  use GenServer
end
```

By adding the use GenServer line, we already have the beginnings of a functioning GenServer.

The GenServer module defines the start_link/3 and start/3 functions for spawning new processes. They take the name of the module to spawn, an initial state, and an optional list of options.

Let's try it out in the console, specifying our new Game module to spawn as well as an empty map for the state.

start_link/3 will return a tagged tuple—{:ok, <PID>} on success and {:error, <reason>} on failure. We can pattern match on the return and bind a variable to the PID on success.

```
$ iex -S mix
. . .
iex> alias IslandsEngine.Game
IslandsEngine.Game

iex> {:ok, pid} = GenServer.start_link(Game, %{})
{:ok, #PID<0.104.0>}
```

Great! We're already able to start the server, and we've hardly written any code.

The GenServer Pattern

There's a simple pattern at the heart of every bit of functionality we build in a GenServer. It has three moving parts—a client function, a function from the GenServer module, and a callback. The client function is the public interface, the part that other processes will call. Within the client function we'll call a GenServer module function that does some internal work before it triggers a callback. The callback is where we do the real work and return a response.

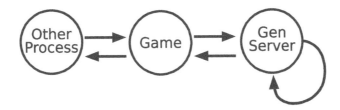

That's the pattern: a client function wraps a GenServer module function, which triggers a callback. We'll see it again and again, both in GenServers and more generally in other OTP Behaviours.

Client functions hold no surprises. They're just everyday Elixir functions. We can name them whatever we want, and they can take any number of arguments.

GenServer defines its own module functions, so we need to abide by their names and arities. GenServer is specific about callback names and arities as well. We can't invent our own.

There's a direct mapping between GenServer module functions and callbacks. Calling GenServer.start_link/3 will always trigger GenServer.init/1. GenServer.call/3 calls GenServer.handle_call/3, and GenServer.cast/2 maps to GenServer.handle_cast/2.

These three pairs of module functions and callbacks are the ones we'll need to build the GenServer for our game.

:gen_server Callbacks

 The Erlang online documentation has a full list of :gen_server module functions and callbacks.[1] In a slightly confusing twist, the docs prepend the callback names with "Module:". These module functions and callbacks handle everything from initializing a process to cleaning up when a process terminates.

Don't worry if this seems abstract at the moment. We'll work through a number of concrete examples in the next few sections.

Passing Messages

The simplest thing we can do with a GenServer is spawn a new server process and send it a message. We've just seen how to spawn a new game server process and bind the resulting PID to a variable. Once we have that PID, we can use Kernel.send/2 to send it a message. Once we have message passing down, we can customize behavior based on that message.

Let's see how this all works.

In a new IEx session, let's start a new game process and send it the message :first:

```
iex> alias IslandsEngine.Game
IslandsEngine.Game

iex> {:ok, game} = GenServer.start_link(Game, %{}, [])
{:ok, #PID<0.128.0>}

iex> send(game, :first)
:first
20:49:47.773 [warn]  IslandsEngine.Game #PID<0.128.0>
                     received unexpected in handle_info/2: :first
```

That worked, after a fashion. At least it didn't crash the IEx process.

---

1. http://erlang.org/doc/man/gen_server.html#Module:code_change-3

The use GenServer line we added to IslandsEngine.Game triggers a macro that compiles default implementations for all of the GenServer callbacks into our Game module. That's why we can actually start the ultra-minimal GenServer we currently have. We'll implement new clauses of these callbacks that override the defaults to fit our needs as we customize the game server.

The warning we got is the compiler's way of telling us we need to implement a clause of the handle_info/2 callback to override the default and match the message we sent.

Let's go ahead and define a handle_info/2 clause in our game server that matches the message :first:

```
def handle_info(:first, state) do
  IO.puts "This message has been handled by handle_info/2, matching on :first."
  {:noreply, state}
end
```

The GenServer module itself provides the second argument, state, when it triggers the handle_info/2 callback. state represents the data structure that the individual GenServer process holds. In this case, we defined it as an empty map when we spawned the process.

The return tuple {:noreply, state} tells the GenServer Behaviour that we don't need to send a message back to the caller, and that the value bound to the state variable should become the new state of the GenServer process. In this case, we haven't transformed the state, so it will still be an empty map.

Now we can recompile Game and try again:

```
iex> {:ok, game} = GenServer.start_link(Game, %{}, [])
{:ok, #PID<0.128.0>}

iex> send(game, :first)
This message has been handled by handle_info/2, matching on :first.
:first
```

That's definitely an improvement over our first try.

Now that we have the idea of sending messages to a GenServer process, let's add a little complexity.

Introducing Calls

More often than not, we're going to want a meaningful response when we send a GenServer process a message. We might query the process's state, or we might want to see the result of a command we've sent it. This is where calls come in.

GenServer calls are synchronous. They can return any arbitrary value to the caller, and if the caller is waiting for a return, it will block until it gets one. The GenServer callback that handles calls is handle_call/3. It's similar to handle_info/2 in that it pattern matches for a message as its first argument.

It's different from handle_info/2 in that it doesn't accept messages sent directly from other processes. Instead, it's triggered whenever we call GenServer.call/2.

Let's try this out. In lib/islands_engine/game.ex add a clause of handle_call/3 that looks like this one. Our aim is to simply have it return the initial server state.

```
def handle_call(:demo_call, _from, state) do
  {:reply, state, state}
end
```

The key here is the first argument, :demo_call. This is the pattern that will determine which clause of handle_call/3 to execute. We'll see where it comes from shortly.

Don't worry about the other arguments. GenServer itself will provide them internally.

The return value is different from the one we used in handle_info/2. It indicates that we'll be replying to the caller. The middle element is the actual reply, and the third element is what we want the state of the GenServer process to be.

Now let's go back to the IEx session we had going and recompile the Game module. Then let's start a new server with %{test: "test value"} as the initial state. Make sure to pattern match on the return so we'll bind the PID to the game variable.

```
iex> {:ok, game} = GenServer.start_link(Game, %{test: "test value"})
{:ok, #PID<0.130.0>}
```

Now invoke GenServer.call/3 with the PID and the atom :demo_call that we specified as the first argument to our clause of handle_call/3. We should get back the state we set when we started the process.

```
iex> GenServer.call(game, :demo_call)
%{test: "test value"}
```

Success! We got the initial state back.

When we invoke GenServer.call/3, GenServer keeps track of the second argument we passed, grabs the PID of the calling process, and gets the process's state. Then it invokes GenServer.handle_call/3 with those arguments, in order:

```
def handle_call(:demo_call, _from, state) do
```

_from is a tuple that contains the PID of the calling process, the IEx session in our case. We could use it to send messages back to the caller, but we don't need to here, so we prepend it with an underscore.

Wait a Minute...

 Our callback returned a tagged tuple, but we only saw the server state in the console. That's because the GenServer processed our callback's return value internally in order to formulate a final reply to the caller. It stripped out the :reply tag and used the final state element to set the new state in the GenServer.

In order to expose this functionality as part of the public interface, we need to define a client function to wrap GenServer.call/3 in lib/islands_engine/game.ex. The only argument it needs is the server PID.

```
def demo_call(game) do
  GenServer.call(game, :demo_call)
end
```

This should behave exactly the same as using GenServer.call/3 directly. Let's try it out. We'll need to recompile the Game module or else start a new session and alias IslandsEngine.Game.

```
iex> {:ok, game} = GenServer.start_link(Game, %{test: "test value"})
{:ok, #PID<0.125.0>}
```

```
iex> Game.demo_call(game)
%{test: "test value"}
```

It returns the server state, which is just what we want.

Introducing Casts

Casts work a lot like calls, so this section will seem familiar. The difference is that casts are asynchronous; they don't return a specific reply, so the caller won't wait for one.

Casts can increase throughput if synchronous processing becomes a bottleneck. But we should prefer calls to casts because they provide a kind of back pressure, limiting the amount of work a process will accept at any given time and preventing it from getting overloaded.

It's good to know how to use casts, though, so we'll practice writing one here. Let's start by defining a handle_cast/2 callback.

We'll have it take a tuple containing the atom :demo_cast as well as a new value we want to set in the state. Then we'll use the Map.put/3 to set a new value for the state's :test key.

Casts don't reply to the calling process, so GenServer won't pass in a reference to it into handle_cast/2.

```
def handle_cast({:demo_cast, new_value}, state) do
  {:noreply, Map.put(state, :test, new_value)}
end
```

We'll return a tagged tuple as our handle_call/3 did. We won't need to reply to the caller, so it will only have two elements—:noreply and the new server state.

To set this up, let's start up a new GenServer and call Game.call_demo/1 with the PID to check the state we have:

```
iex> {:ok, game} = GenServer.start_link(Game, %{test: "test value"})
{:ok, #PID<0.130.0>}

iex> Game.demo_call(game)
%{test: "test value"}
```

We get the initial state back, which is what we expect.

Now let's run the cast, followed by the call to return the state. If all goes well, we should get the new state back:

```
iex> GenServer.cast(game, {:demo_cast, "another value"})
:ok

iex> Game.demo_call(game)
%{test: "another value"}
```

Indeed, the cast did work.

We can wrap the GenServer.cast/2 call in a client function, and it should behave the same as the bare GenServer.cast/2 call.

```
def demo_cast(pid, new_value) do
  GenServer.cast(pid, {:demo_cast, new_value})
end
```

Now that we have the basics down, we can delete the handle_info/2, handle_call/3, and handle_cast/2 callbacks as well as the demo_call/1 and demo_cast/2 functions. We won't need them for the rest of our work here.

Initializing GenServer State

Until now, we've relied directly on GenServer's built-in start_link/3 function for starting new processes. This works, but we can do better.

When we run GenServer.start_link(Game, <initial state>), the idea that we're starting a new *game* process is buried in the arguments. It would be much clearer if we could bring the Game module out front by writing Game.start_link(<initial state>).

To do this, we'll follow the GenServer pattern—define a public function that wraps a GenServer module function that triggers a callback.

Let's start with a public start_link/1 function in the Game module and have it wrap the GenServer.start_link/3 function. One player will start the game, and the second will join later. Let's have Game.start_link/1 take the first player's name in order to help build the state we'll need.

While we're at it, let's add a guard to make sure the name is a string:

```
def start_link(name) when is_binary(name), do:
  GenServer.start_link(__MODULE__, name, [])
```

We've used __MODULE__, a macro which returns the name of the current module, instead of hard-coding the module name. That will avoid errors if we ever change the module name.

GenServer uses the middle argument, in this case name, as the only argument to the callback that GenServer.start_link/3 triggers, init/1.

The third argument is an optional list of options. We'll take advantage of it later on when we work on naming GenServer processes.

This public function has greater significance than its single line might suggest. This is the beginning of the public interface for a game. It allows other processes to programmatically start new game processes.

Currently, we've built two thirds of the GenServer pattern—the public function and the GenServer module function. The remaining part is the init/1 callback. Let's define that next.

We'll be working with some new modules in this function, so let's alias them up front:

```
alias IslandsEngine.{Board, Guesses, Rules}
```

The general form of init/1 is to pattern match on an argument, perform any necessary initializations, and return a tagged tuple of the form {:ok, initial_state}.

GenServer provides the name argument, and our job is to use it to help build the state we'll need to play the game.

Islands requires two players for each game. Each player needs a name, a board, and guesses representing their opponent's board. The game itself needs a rules struct so it can manage the game.

We can model the structure of that state with a couple of maps.

```
gen_server/lib/islands_engine/game.ex
def init(name) do
  player1 = %{name: name, board: Board.new(), guesses: Guesses.new()}
  player2 = %{name: nil,  board: Board.new(), guesses: Guesses.new()}
  {:ok, %{player1: player1, player2: player2, rules: %Rules{}}}
end
```

Notice we only set the name for the first player. One player starts the game. We'll show how we'll add the second player in a bit. Let's see it in action.

In a new console session, first alias IslandsEngine.Game.

```
iex> alias IslandsEngine.Game
IslandsEngine.Game
```

Then start a new game with the username "Frank," binding the variable game to the new game PID along the way:

```
iex> {:ok, game} = Game.start_link("Frank")
{:ok, #PID<0.99.0>}
```

The Erlang :sys module includes a function called get_state/1 that will return the state of a :gen_server process. It's not intended for use in production code, but it's perfect for debugging, testing, and general exploring like we're doing here.

```
iex> state_data = :sys.get_state(game)
%{player1: %{board: %{},
    guesses: %IslandsEngine.Guesses{hits: #MapSet<[]>, misses: #MapSet<[]>},
    name: "Frank"},
  player2: %{board: %{},
    guesses: %IslandsEngine.Guesses{hits: #MapSet<[]>, misses: #MapSet<[]>},
    name: nil},
  rules: %IslandsEngine.Rules{player1: :islands_not_set,
   player2: :islands_not_set, state: :initialized}}
```

This is what we're looking for. We've got two player maps and a rules struct set in the game's state.

Now let's make sure that we actually set the first player's name when we started the game:

```
iex> state_data.player1.name
"Frank"
```

Which it did; that's exactly what we want.

Customizing GenServer Behavior

Spawning and initializing a new GenServer process is a great start, but the default callback implementations we got with use GenServer don't go very far.

In order to build real applications, we need to change the way a GenServer behaves to fit each application's needs.

To do this, we're going to follow the pattern we've used so far—write a client function that wraps a GenServer function that triggers a callback. The callback is where we'll define the new behavior.

Each time we add a new public function, we build a new piece of the interface for the game. As we go along, we'll expose more and more of the game's behavior. This interface acts as a boundary between the rest of the system and a game. That makes it the exact right place to check any values passed into the public functions.

In each of the callbacks, we'll need to check some conditions before we can determine whether the action went as planned. At a minimum, we'll need to check the rules for each action. Additionally, we might have to check that coordinates and islands are valid or that a player has positioned all his islands.

We could do this with conditional logic, but that could easily turn into a mess. Instead, we will rely on Elixir's with/1 special form. with/1 was designed to test multiple conditions in the same place, in a sane way, without nested conditionals.

Each time we use with/1, we'll employ the same three blocks. The with block will contain all the conditions we're testing. The do block is for the actions we'll take when all the conditions pass, and the else block is where we'll handle errors.

Besides starting a new game, there are four behaviors we need to define: adding a second player, positioning islands, setting islands, and guessing coordinates. We'll handle them in that order.

Let's get to it.

Add a New Player

Each game will need to add a second player in order to begin play. This really amounts to assigning a value to the :name key for the second player.

We'll begin with a public client function, add_player/2, which will take the PID of the game process and the second player's name. We'll have add_player/2 wrap GenServer.call/2 so that it will be synchronous. Then we'll need a new clause of handle_call/3 to define the new behavior.

gen_server/lib/islands_engine/game.ex

```
def add_player(game, name) when is_binary(name), do:
  GenServer.call(game, {:add_player, name})
```

We've added a guard clause here to make sure the name is a string.

Next up is a handle_call/3 clause that pattern matches for the {:add_player, name} tuple we passed into GenServer.call/3:

```
def handle_call({:add_player, name}, _from, state_data) do
```

There's only one condition we need to check for in the with block: whether the rules allow us to add another player:

```
with
  {:ok, rules} <- Rules.check(state_data.rules, :add_player)
```

When the result of Rules.check/2 matches {:ok, rules}, we'll have some work to do in the do block. We'll need to transform the game state by updating player2's name, updating the rules struct, and sending a reply back to the caller.

That sounds like it's just made for a pipeline:

```
do
  state_data
  |> update_player2_name(name)
  |> update_rules(rules)
  |> reply_success(:ok)
```

That pipeline calls some functions we don't currently have, but we'll get to those in a minute.

The only error we would expect to see from the with block is :error if the rules didn't allow the action. Let's handle that in the else block:

```
else
  :error -> {:reply, :error, state_data}
end
```

Now let's fill in the missing functions from the pipeline. These will all be private functions. The first one we'll need will be one to update the player's name in the state data:

gen_server/lib/islands_engine/game.ex
```
defp update_player2_name(state_data, name), do:
  put_in(state_data.player2.name, name)
```

Kernel.put_in/2 is a great choice here because it will transform values nested in a map and return the whole, transformed map. The next thing we'll need to do is set the transformed rules struct back in the state data:

gen_server/lib/islands_engine/game.ex
```
defp update_rules(state_data, rules), do: %{state_data | rules: rules}
```

The map update syntax is fine for this.

The last thing we need to do is send a reply tuple. We've got a nice pipeline going here, so let's keep it going with a function that takes the transformed state data as well as a reply value and crafts a reply tuple from those.

gen_server/lib/islands_engine/game.ex
```
defp reply_success(state_data, reply), do: {:reply, reply, state_data}
```

When we put all three blocks together, the whole clause of handle_call/3 looks like this:

gen_server/lib/islands_engine/game.ex
```
def handle_call({:add_player, name}, _from, state_data) do
  with {:ok, rules} <- Rules.check(state_data.rules, :add_player)
  do
    state_data
    |> update_player2_name(name)
    |> update_rules(rules)
    |> reply_success(:ok)
  else
    :error -> {:reply, :error, state_data}
  end
end
```

Let's see it in action. In a new console session, let's alias IslandsEngine.Game and start a new game server:

```
iex> alias IslandsEngine.Game
IslandsEngine.Game
```

```
iex> {:ok, game} = Game.start_link("Frank")
{:ok, #PID<0.99.0>}
```

Now let's try to add a second player:

```
iex> Game.add_player(game, "Dweezil")
:ok
```

That seemed to work, so let's check the data:

```
iex> state_data = :sys.get_state(game)
. . .
```

```
iex> state_data.player2.name
"Dweezil"
```

Yay! It works.

Now that we can add a second player, it's time to handle positioning islands.

Position Islands

When players move their islands around on the board, the UI will send messages back to the server. Those messages will include a key for the island type as well as the row and column numbers for the upper-left coordinate of the island.

The Board module knows how to position an island with a key and a full island. The Coordinate module can turn the row and column value into a coordinate, and the Island module can turn the island key and the coordinate into a full island. The Game module will coordinate between these, check to see that all the values are valid, and formulate a response.

Since we'll be working with boards, islands, and coordinates, let's add those modules to our list of aliases:

```
alias IslandsEngine.{Board, Coordinate, Guesses, Island, Rules}
```

We'll start with a public function for the interface as we have before. It will take the game process PID, the player, the island key, as well as the row and column of the island's upper-left coordinate. We'll use GenServer.call/2 so that we can send a response back to the caller.

We will want to make sure that the value we get for the player matches either :player1 or :player2. Let's add a module attribute with both those atoms in a list:

```
@players [:player1, :player2]
```

Now we can add a guard for that in the function head:

gen_server/lib/islands_engine/game.ex
```
def position_island(game, player, key, row, col) when player in @players, do:
  GenServer.call(game, {:position_island, player, key, row, col})
```

For the rest of the game, we'll need to work with individual players' boards, so let's define a convenience function for extracting them from the game state:

gen_server/lib/islands_engine/game.ex
```
defp player_board(state_data, player), do: Map.get(state_data, player).board
```

With that, we're ready to define the handle_call/3 callback for positioning islands.

For success, we need to check a number of conditions:

- that the rules permit players to position their islands
- that the row and col values generate a valid coordinate
- that the island key and the upper-left coordinate generate a valid island
- that positioning the island doesn't generate an error

This is where with/1 really shows its power. In most languages we would need a tangle of conditionals to check for the success of all of these. Those checks might be physically separated from one another, so we would lose the overall picture of what we're checking for.

Using with/1, we put all the checks in one place. We see the whole story at a glance, and we can do all the error handling in a single else block as well:

```
with  {:ok, rules} <-
        Rules.check(state_data.rules, {:position_islands, player}),
      {:ok, coordinate} <-
        Coordinate.new(row, col),
      {:ok, island} <-
        Island.new(key, coordinate),
      %{} = board <-
        Board.position_island(board, key, island)
```

These checks all rely on pattern matching, so order is important. The first pattern that doesn't match will halt the execution.

In our case, the rules check comes first. If the rules say that the action isn't allowed, there's no reason to do any of the other checks.

Similarly, we need to make sure that the row and col values generate a valid coordinate before we use that coordinate to generate an island. If the island is invalid, there's no point trying to position it.

If there are no errors to this point, Board.position_island/2 has already done the work. All that's left is to update the game state.

Rules.check/2 returns a transformed rules struct, and Board.position_island/2 returns a transformed board map. We'll need to reset both of those as well as send a reply indicating success.

```
do
  state_data
  |> update_board(player, board)
  |> update_rules(rules)
  |> reply_success(:ok)
```

We've already defined functions to update the rules and to return a successful reply. The one we need now is the one to update the board:

gen_server/lib/islands_engine/game.ex
```
defp update_board(state_data, player, board), do:
  Map.update!(state_data, player, fn player -> %{player | board: board} end)
```

That's the happy path, but we need to handle errors as well. We want to be specific about the possible errors we can encounter. If we get anything that's not in the list of normal errors, that would be exceptional and we should let the process throw an error and crash.

```
else
  :error ->
    {:reply, :error, state_data}
  {:error, :invalid_coordinate} ->
    {:reply, {:error, :invalid_coordinate}, state_data}
  {:error, :invalid_island_type} ->
    {:reply, {:error, :invalid_island_type}, state_data}
end
```

Putting all the pieces together, we get the full clause of handle_call/3:

```
gen_server/lib/islands_engine/game.ex
def handle_call({:position_island, player, key, row, col}, _from, state_data)
do
  board = player_board(state_data, player)
  with  {:ok, rules} <-
          Rules.check(state_data.rules, {:position_islands, player}),
        {:ok, coordinate} <-
          Coordinate.new(row, col),
        {:ok, island} <-
          Island.new(key, coordinate),
        %{} = board <-
          Board.position_island(board, key, island)
  do
    state_data
    |> update_board(player, board)
    |> update_rules(rules)
    |> reply_success(:ok)
  else
    :error -> {:reply, :error, state_data}
    {:error, :invalid_coordinate} ->
      {:reply, {:error, :invalid_coordinate}, state_data}
    {:error, :invalid_island_type} ->
      {:reply, {:error, :invalid_island_type}, state_data}
  end
end
```

Let's take it out for a spin to see how it behaves. We'll take a look at the happy path first.

We'll need to alias all the modules we'll use, start a new game process, and add a second player so that the game will be in the :players_set state:

```
iex> alias IslandsEngine.{Game, Rules}
[IslandsEngine.Game, IslandsEngine.Rules]

iex> {:ok, game} = Game.start_link("Fred")
{:ok, #PID<0.115.0>}

iex> Game.add_player(game, "Wilma")
:ok
```

```
iex> state_data = :sys.get_state(game)
. . .
```

```
iex> state_data.rules.state
:players_set
```

Then we should be able to have player1 position a square island beginning at row 1 and column 1:

```
iex> Game.position_island(game, :player1, :square, 1, 1)
:ok
```

```
iex> state_data = :sys.get_state(game)
. . .
```

```
iex> state_data.player1.board
%{square:
  %IslandsEngine.Island{
    coordinates: #MapSet<[
      %IslandsEngine.Coordinate{col: 1, row: 1},
      %IslandsEngine.Coordinate{col: 1, row: 2},
      %IslandsEngine.Coordinate{col: 2, row: 1},
      %IslandsEngine.Coordinate{col: 2, row: 2}
    ]>,
    hit_coordinates: #MapSet<[]>
  }
}
```

Fantastic. That's just what we want.

If we try to position an island with an invalid row or column, we should get an :invalid_coordinate error:

```
iex> Game.position_island(game, :player1, :dot, 12, 1)
{:error, :invalid_coordinate}
```

Great—that's what we do get.

If we pass in an invalid island key, we should get an :invalid_island_type error:

```
iex> Game.position_island(game, :player1, :wrong, 1, 1)
{:error, :invalid_island_type}
```

Perfect. Now let's try positioning an island with a valid row and column that will generate a coordinate that's off the board. That should also return an :invalid_coordinate error:

```
iex> Game.position_island(game, :player1, :l_shape, 10, 10)
{:error, :invalid_coordinate}
```

Nice.

There's one more type of error we might regularly run into: when the rules don't allow the action. To try this, we can use Erlang's :sys.replace_state/2 function. It takes the PID of the process to replace the state for, and an anonymous function that returns the new state to use.

Let's set our game process to :player1_turn, where neither player should be able to position islands anymore:

```
iex> state_data = :sys.replace_state(game, fn state_data ->
...>   %{state_data | rules: %Rules{state: :player1_turn}}
...> end)
. . .

iex> state_data.rules.state
:player1_turn
```

That looks correct. With the new state set, we should get a plain :error back:

```
iex> Game.position_island(game, :player1, :dot, 5, 5)
:error
```

That's perfect. The happy path works, and we get the errors we expect when we expect them.

Let's move on to setting islands next.

Set Islands

Once the players are done positioning their islands, they mark them as set. After that, they can no longer move them around the board.

The game itself doesn't track this. Only the Rules module knows whether players have set their islands. But the Board module has a role to play in the decision. It knows whether or not players have positioned all their islands.

The Rules module cares that the state is in :players_set, and it cares that players have not already set their islands.

The decision as to whether players should be able to set their islands depends partly on the Rules and partly on the Board—whether or not players have positioned all their islands.

We'll test these two conditions in our with/1 clause. Let's begin with public interface function set_islands/2. Since this action is per player, we'll need it to take the player as an argument in addition to the game PID:

```
gen_server/lib/islands_engine/game.ex
def set_islands(game, player) when player in @players, do:
  GenServer.call(game, {:set_islands, player})
```

There are two conditions we need to check for here. The first is that the rules allow the player to set his islands. The second is that the player has already positioned all of his islands on the board.

```
with {:ok, rules} <- Rules.check(state_data.rules, {:set_islands, player}),
     true          <- Board.all_islands_positioned?(board)
```

We don't transform any information in the board during this operation, but we do in the rules struct. When both of these conditions are met, all we need to do is update the rules in the state data and send a successful response.

That successful response will include the board with all its islands. This will only go to the player who set her islands, and it will make it easy for the front-end code to represent the full board.

```
do
  state_data
  |> update_rules(rules)
  |> reply_success({:ok, board})
```

There are two errors that we would expect to encounter: one with the rules, :error, and another if not all of a player's islands are set, false.

```
else
  :error -> {:reply, :error, state_data}
  false  -> {:reply, {:error, :not_all_islands_positioned}, state_data}
end
```

When we assemble all the pieces, this is what we get:

```
gen_server/lib/islands_engine/game.ex
def handle_call({:set_islands, player}, _from, state_data) do
  board = player_board(state_data, player)
  with {:ok, rules} <- Rules.check(state_data.rules, {:set_islands, player}),
       true          <- Board.all_islands_positioned?(board)
  do
    state_data
    |> update_rules(rules)
    |> reply_success({:ok, board})
  else
    :error -> {:reply, :error, state_data}
    false  -> {:reply, {:error, :not_all_islands_positioned}, state_data}
  end
end
```

Let's try this out in the console.

We'll need to alias the Game and Rules modules and then start a new game server process:

```
iex> alias IslandsEngine.Game
IslandsEngine.Game

iex> {:ok, game} = Game.start_link("Dino")
{:ok, #PID<0.115.0>}
```

Then we'll need to add a second player in order to transition the state to :players_set:

```
iex> Game.add_player(game, "Pebbles")
:ok
```

At this point, if we try to set player1's islands, we should get an error because even though the game is in the correct state, player1 hasn't positioned all her islands yet:

```
iex> Game.set_islands(game, :player1)
{:error, :not_all_islands_positioned}
```

That's the exact error we do get. Let's fix that by positioning each of the islands so that they don't overlap:

```
iex> Game.position_island(game, :player1, :atoll, 1, 1)
:ok

iex> Game.position_island(game, :player1, :dot, 1, 4)
:ok

iex> Game.position_island(game, :player1, :l_shape, 1, 5)
:ok

iex> Game.position_island(game, :player1, :s_shape, 5, 1)
:ok

iex> Game.position_island(game, :player1, :square, 5, 5)
:ok
```

Now when we try to set player1's islands, we should be successful:

```
iex> Game.set_islands(game, :player1)
{:ok,
 %{atoll: %IslandsEngine.Island{
         coordinates: #MapSet<[
            %IslandsEngine.Coordinate{col: 1, row: 1},
            %IslandsEngine.Coordinate{col: 1, row: 3},
            %IslandsEngine.Coordinate{col: 2, row: 1},
            %IslandsEngine.Coordinate{col: 2, row: 2},
            %IslandsEngine.Coordinate{col: 2, row: 3}
         ]>,
         hit_coordinates: #MapSet<[]>
       },
 . . .
}}
```

We are. That's great!

Let's check the game's state data to make sure we're still in the :players_set state and that the rules struct knows that player1 has set her islands:

```
iex> state_data = :sys.get_state(game)
. . .
iex> state_data.rules.player1
:islands_set
iex> state_data.rules.state
:players_set
```

That all works as it should. The next thing we need to tackle is guessing a coordinate.

Guess a Coordinate

Guessing coordinates is the most important action in the game of Islands. In order to process a guess, we'll need to know which player is doing the guessing as well as the row and column values that the player is guessing.

We'll start with a client function, guess_coordinate/4, that takes those values. That will wrap a GenServer.call/2 with a tuple representing the four arguments and the action:

gen_server/lib/islands_engine/game.ex
```
def guess_coordinate(game, player, row, col) when player in @players, do:
  GenServer.call(game, {:guess_coordinate, player, row, col})
```

One of the tricky things to remember about guessing is that players guess against their opponent's board. Let's write a convenience function for getting the key of a player's opponent. From there, we can get the opponent's board with player_board/1.

gen_server/lib/islands_engine/game.ex
```
defp opponent(:player1), do: :player2
defp opponent(:player2), do: :player1
```

We'll need to check a number of conditions—whether:

- the rules allow the given player to guess

- the row and column values make a valid coordinate

- the guess was a hit or a miss, whether it forested an island, and whether it won the game

- the state should transition to :game_over

Those checks define our with block:

```
with {:ok, rules} <-
       Rules.check(state_data.rules, {:guess_coordinate, player_key}),
     {:ok, coordinate} <-
       Coordinate.new(row, col),
     {hit_or_miss, forested_island, win_status, opponent_board} <-
       Board.guess(opponent_board, coordinate),
     {:ok, rules} <-
       Rules.check(rules, {:win_check, win_status})
```

In the cases where all of those checks pass, we'll need to update the state data and the rules struct. We'll have to add the current guess to the guessing player's guesses.

We'll also go ahead and update the opponent's board because a hit would transform an island by adding a coordinate to the :hit_coordinates set.

We are making a trade-off here by adding an extra operation for some cases in order to eliminate the complexity of checking whether the guess was a hit. That informs what we need to put in the pipeline of the do block:

```
do
  state_data
  |> update_board(opponent_key, opponent_board)
  |> update_guesses(player_key, hit_or_miss, coordinate)
  |> update_rules(rules)
  |> reply_success({hit_or_miss, forested_island, win_status})
```

There's one new function in this pipeline: update_guesses/4. The Guesses module provides the add/3 function; the problem is that each player's guesses struct is two layers deep in the state data. We could extract that struct manually, transform it, and put it back, but there's an easier way. Elixir's Kernel.update_in/2 allows us to easily update nested data:

gen_server/lib/islands_engine/game.ex
```
defp update_guesses(state_data, player_key, hit_or_miss, coordinate) do
  update_in(state_data[player_key].guesses, fn guesses ->
    Guesses.add(guesses, hit_or_miss, coordinate)
  end)
end
```

The first argument to update_in/2 is the path to the data. The second is an anonymous function to do the transformation.

There are only two error conditions we should see from all this: when the rules say an action isn't allowed, and when the row and column values generate an invalid coordinate. We'll cover those in the else block. Any other error will raise, as it should.

```
else
  :error ->
    {:reply, :error, state_data}
  {:error, :invalid_coordinate} ->
    {:reply, {:error, :invalid_coordinate}, state_data}
end
```

Now let's put all those pieces together into a single clause of handle_call/3:

gen_server/lib/islands_engine/game.ex

```
def handle_call({:guess_coordinate, player_key, row, col}, _from, state_data)
do
  opponent_key = opponent(player_key)
  opponent_board = player_board(state_data, opponent_key)

  with {:ok, rules} <-
         Rules.check(state_data.rules, {:guess_coordinate, player_key}),
       {:ok, coordinate} <-
         Coordinate.new(row, col),
       {hit_or_miss, forested_island, win_status, opponent_board} <-
         Board.guess(opponent_board, coordinate),
       {:ok, rules} <-
         Rules.check(rules, {:win_check, win_status})
  do
    state_data
    |> update_board(opponent_key, opponent_board)
    |> update_guesses(player_key, hit_or_miss, coordinate)
    |> update_rules(rules)
    |> reply_success({hit_or_miss, forested_island, win_status})
  else
    :error ->
      {:reply, :error, state_data}
    {:error, :invalid_coordinate} ->
      {:reply, {:error, :invalid_coordinate}, state_data}
  end
end
```

Let's try this out in the console:

```
iex> alias IslandsEngine.{Game, Rules}
[IslandsEngine.Game, IslandsEngine.Rules]
```

```
iex> {:ok, game} = Game.start_link("Miles")
{:ok, #PID<0.129.0>}
```

If we try guessing a coordinate right away, Rules.check/2 should return :error because the game is still in the :initialized state:

```
iex> Game.guess_coordinate(game, :player1, 1, 1)
:error
```

That's exactly the error we get.

Now let's add a second player and position an island for both players:

```
iex> Game.add_player(game, "Trane")
:ok

iex> Game.position_island(game, :player1, :dot, 1, 1)
:ok

iex> Game.position_island(game, :player2, :square, 1, 1)
:ok
```

To save some time, let's cut a corner and manually set the state to :player1_turn:

```
iex> state_data = :sys.get_state(game)
. . .

iex> state_data = :sys.replace_state(game, fn data ->
...>   %{state_data | rules: %Rules{state: :player1_turn}}
...> end)
. . .

iex> state_data.rules.state
:player1_turn
```

Let's have :player1 guess a wrong coordinate. The response we get should be {:miss, :none, :no_win}:

```
iex> Game.guess_coordinate(game, :player1, 5, 5)
{:miss, :none, :no_win}
```

That's perfect.

If :player1 tries to guess again, the rules should catch that and return :error:

```
iex> Game.guess_coordinate(game, :player1, 3, 1)
:error
```

Excellent! That was just what we expected.

If :player2 guesses the single coordinate in :dot island, he should win the game:

```
iex> Game.guess_coordinate(game, :player2, 1, 1)
{:hit, :dot, :win}
```

That's exactly what happens.

With that, we've defined the interface and all the behavior we'll need from the Game module. The last thing we'll need is to be able to address each game process by name in the system.

Naming GenServer Processes

This whole chapter we've been starting new GenServer processes and binding their PIDs to variables. Whenever we've needed to call a public function on a process, we've passed that variable in as the first argument. That clearly works, but it leaves us with a problem.

In a full application, we'd need to keep track of every variable for every process we started. We'd need to always keep them in scope, and we'd need to clear individual variables out when their process stopped. If that sounds really messy, it is.

It would be great if we could just name each process as we start it, and pass that name in whenever we wanted to call a function. It would be even better if we didn't have to remember the name, but were able to reconstruct it on the fly when we needed to. If wishes came true, these names would clear themselves out when their process stopped.

Wishes can come true. Process registration will do all of this for us.

There are several ways to register GenServer processes by name. Let's explore them and see which best fits our needs.

The first thing we can do is simply specify a name as an atom as the third argument to GenServer.start_link/3. Let's open up a new console to test that out:

```
iex> alias IslandsEngine.Game
IslandsEngine.Game

iex> GenServer.start_link(Game, "Frank", name: :islands_game)
{:ok, #PID<0.90.0>}
```

We are fine using the raw GenServer.start_link/3 function here. We need to specify the module name instead of using __MODULE__ because this function call is not originating inside the Game module the way it is in IslandsEngine.Game.start_link/1.

The part to watch is the keyword list we specified as the third argument, name: :islands_game. This clearly works. We get {:ok, #PID<0.90.0>} as the return value.

Now we can use the atom :islands_game instead of a PID whenever we call client functions in the Game module:

```
iex> :sys.get_state(:islands_game)
%{player1: %{board: %{},
    guesses: %IslandsEngine.Guesses{hits: #MapSet<[]>, misses: #MapSet<[]>},
    name: "Frank"},
  player2: %{board: %{},
    guesses: %IslandsEngine.Guesses{hits: #MapSet<[]>, misses: #MapSet<[]>},
    name: nil},
  rules: %IslandsEngine.Rules{player1: :islands_not_set,
   player2: :islands_not_set, state: :initialized}}
```

The atom has a direct one-to-one mapping to the PID of a single game process. If we try to start another one with the same atom for the name, we get an error saying that the server is already running:

```
iex> GenServer.start_link(Game, "Frank", name: :islands_game)
{:error, {:already_started, #PID<0.90.0>}}
```

Using Process Registration to Our Advantage

 This property of naming GenServers can be useful. If we ever need to enforce that there be only a single instance of a given GenServer, we can name it with a hard-coded atom. The Erlang virtual machine will not allow more than one GenServer of that type to start up.

This type of process registration is called a local name. It is visible only on the same node on which the process is spawned, and the name must be an atom.

This leads to a problem for our use case. In Islands, we'll be spinning up a new game process for each pair of players. Elixir doesn't garbage-collect atoms, so the list of atoms will grow as we spawn more games. The BEAM enforces a hard limit of about a million atoms. If we reach that limit, the whole node will crash, no exceptions. Those are the kinds of things that trigger system alerts in the middle of the night.

We might also register a process name as a string with Erlang's global name service. This requires hardly any change at all. We just specify the value of the name as a tagged tuple.

The one bit of data we have whenever we start a new game is the first player's name. That's a value we'll have around as long as the game exists, and it's perfect to construct a name with.

```
iex> GenServer.start_link(Game, "Frank", name: {:global, "game:Frank"})
{:ok, #PID<0.137.0>}
```

The global registry won't let us register the same string for a new process. If we try, we get the same error as when we tried to register the same local name twice.

The global name registry works across all connected nodes in the system. If we add more nodes, they will automatically know about—and be able to use—the globally registered processes. It will also take care of remapping PIDs when supervisors restart their processes as well as removing entries for terminated processes.

This functionality comes at a cost, though. There is overhead associated with keeping track of processes across nodes. Global registration can be the right choice when our application runs on multiple nodes, but there are other choices when we're working in a single-node environment.

The :via Option

If we want, we can define our own module to register process names in any way that fits our purpose. Any module that defines register_name/2, unregister_name/1, whereis_name/1, and send/2 will do. With a module like that in place, we can register our process name with {:via, module_name, term_for_name}. :global is the name of one such module that happens to be built into Erlang.

As of Elixir 1.4, there is another path to process registration: the Registry module. In order to use it, we need to have a via tuple. That's a three-element tuple tagged with :via. The middle element is the module that will register processes, Registry, and the third element is the key to register the processes under. We'll use the tuple {Registry.Game, name}.

Typing this via tuple out whenever we'll need it would get old pretty fast, so let's write a function to do it for us:

gen_server/lib/islands_engine/game.ex
```
def via_tuple(name), do: {:via, Registry, {Registry.Game, name}}
```

We can use that function to name each process in Game.start_link/1:

gen_server/lib/islands_engine/game.ex
```
def start_link(name) when is_binary(name), do:
  GenServer.start_link(__MODULE__, name, name: via_tuple(name))
```

There's one last step to make this work. We'll need to start a Registry process when we start the IslandsEngine application.

Open up lib/islands_engine/application.ex and look for the start/2 function. Inside start/2, you'll see an empty list bound to the children variable. Go ahead and add {Registry, keys: :unique, name: Registry.Game)} to that list:

```
children = [
  {Registry, keys: :unique, name: Registry.Game}
]
```

We'll talk about supervisors in the next chapter. For now, know that this line will start the Registry, and specify that keys should be unique for the Registry.Game module. We don't need to further define the Registry.Game module. This will simply work. The reason it'll work is that in Elixir, module names are just atoms.

```
iex> :"Elixir.Registry.Game" == Registry.Game
true
```

That makes the third element of our via tuple equal to {:"Elixir.Registry.Game", name}. That's just a tagged tuple used as a key that maps to the game PID.

Let's see how this works in the console:

```
iex> alias IslandsEngine.Game
IslandsEngine.Game

iex> via = Game.via_tuple("Lena")
{:via, Registry, {Registry.Game, "Lena"}}

iex> GenServer.start_link(Game, "Lena", name: via)
{:ok, #PID<0.119.0>}

iex> :sys.get_state(via)
%{player1: %{board: %{},
    guesses: %IslandsEngine.Guesses{hits: #MapSet<[]>, misses: #MapSet<[]>},
    name: "Lena"},
  player2: %{board: %{},
    guesses: %IslandsEngine.Guesses{hits: #MapSet<[]>, misses: #MapSet<[]>},
    name: nil},
  rules: %IslandsEngine.Rules{player1: :islands_not_set,
    player2: :islands_not_set, state: :initialized}}

iex> GenServer.start_link(Game, "Lena", name: via)
{:error, {:already_started, #PID<0.119.0>}}
```

That's fantastic—just what we need.

With that, our GenServer is complete. Starting with a new module, we've seen how to start new GenServer processes, initialize state, customize behavior, and name individual processes.

Wrapping Up

You've come a long way in this chapter.

You've learned about OTP Behaviours. That knowledge will stand you in good stead for the next few chapters. More importantly, it'll come in handy whenever we're building applications in Elixir.

We showed you how to build a custom GenServer. We drilled the pattern of client function wrapping a GenServer function, which triggers a callback, into your head. And you saw how to register names to individual GenServer processes so that they are addressable from anywhere.

The game itself has come a long way. We've built an interface that allows any external process to play the game. At this point, the game is nearly complete. The question we have to answer next is, what happens when things go wrong?

What we'll do in this chapter

  - *look at linking process and trapping exits*
  - *examine the strategies for process supervision*
  - *build a custom supervisor*
  - *restore game state after a crash*

CHAPTER 5

Process Supervision for Recovery

We all work with computers. We know it's inevitable that things will go wrong, sometimes really wrong. In spite of our best laid plans, state goes bad, systems raise exceptions, and servers crash. These failures often seem to come out of nowhere, unpredictably and without warning.

To combat these inevitable problems, we need to boost fault tolerance. We need to isolate failures as much as possible, handle them, and have the system as a whole carry on.

Elixir and OTP provide a world-class mechanism for handling problems and moving on: process supervision. Process supervision means we can have specialized processes that watch other processes, and restart them when they crash.

The mechanism we use to define and spawn these specialized processes is the supervisor.

We're going to build our own supervisor for the Game module. We'll make sure it starts a new process when we start the game engine. We'll use that supervisor process to start and supervise each game process.

Along the way, we'll look at some ideas about fault tolerance, examine different ways we can spawn processes in Elixir, and take a really good look at the supervisor Behaviour.

The first step in this path is understanding the ways different languages provide fault tolerance.

Fault Tolerance

Erlang and Elixir have reputations for tremendous fault tolerance. This is well deserved, but not because they prevent errors. Instead they give us the tools to recover gracefully from any errors that crop up at runtime.

Almost all languages, including Elixir, have built-in mechanisms to handle exceptions. These require that we identify risky code in advance, wrap it in a block that tries to execute it, and provide a block to rescue the situation if the code fails. In most languages, this kind of exception handling is essential, but in Elixir we hardly ever have to reach for it.

The OTP team at Ericsson took an interesting tack around this pattern. For them, extreme fault tolerance wasn't a "nice to have." It was a critical requirement of the language. Telephone utilities have very stringent uptime requirements. The phones need to work no matter what, even in the event of a natural disaster.

The team reasoned that it's nearly impossible to predict all possible failures in advance, so they decided to focus on recovering from failure instead. They wanted to code for the happy path and have a separate mechanism get things back on track when the inevitable errors happen.

The design they came up with is the supervisor Behaviour. It extracts error handling code from business logic into its own modules. Supervisor modules spawn supervisor processes that link to other processes and watch for failure, restarting those linked processes if they crash.

This separation of concerns makes our code clearer and easier to maintain. It keeps our business logic free of diversions for handling exceptions. We end up writing more confident code that assumes success, but supervisors always have our back when things go wrong.

The supervisor Behaviour is based on ideas that build on and reinforce each other:

1) Most runtime errors are transient and happen because of bad state.

2) The best way to fix bad state is to let the process crash and restart it with good state.

3) Restarts works best on systems like the BEAM that have small, independent processes. Having independent processes lets us isolate errors to the smallest area possible, minimizing any disruption during restarts.

History shows the OTP team's approach is more effective than exception handling. We've built more fault-tolerant systems not because we anticipated specific errors, but because we have the tools to recover gracefully from all errors when they inevitably crop up.

We're going to look at process supervision from all angles. We'll start with the different ways we can spawn new processes and the implications that has for how processes interact. That will lead us to the way supervisors interact with the processes they supervise. We'll see the different strategies supervisors can use for restarting crashed processes, and then we'll talk about different ways of recovering state after processes restart.

To illustrate how process supervision works, let's start with the different ways we can spawn processes and the effect those different ways have on the way processes interact.

Linking Processes

Supervisors may sound magical, but there are two simple, practical mechanisms behind their magic: linking processes and trapping exits. We're going to see how they work together to make supervisors work.

The key to process supervision is for one process to be able to link to other processes and know when those other processes crash. Beyond that, the supervising process needs to be able to keep running if it gets crash notifications from processes it's linked to.

When one process in a group of linked processes crashes, it sends a special kind of message called an exit signal to all the other processes it's linked to. Any process that receives an exit signal will also exit and send an exit signal to all the other processes that it is linked to, forming a kind of chain reaction of exits.

This chain reaction makes it hard to fulfill one of the main ideas behind supervisor processes—which is not to crash—when one of the processes they're monitoring does crash.

The mechanism to fix this is called trapping exits. When a process traps exits, it transforms exit signals into regular messages that end up in the process's mailbox. That process can then handle those regular messages just as it would any other. That's the key to making supervisors work.

Those are nice words, and they help us understand supervisors from one angle, but digging in and watching processes interact in the console will deepen our understanding. That's what we're about to do.

Sending and Receiving Messages

We're going to see how unlinked processes behave when they exit. Then we'll do the same for linked processes as well as linked processes where one is trapping exits.

Much of this work involves passing and retrieving messages directly. We'll use send/2 to send messages and receive/1 to pull them from a process's mailbox.

Let's take a quick practice run with these functions in IEx.

The first step is to check the IEx process PID with self/0:

```
iex> self()
#PID<0.122.0>
```

Next, we can have IEx send itself a message, "Hello World!":

```
iex> send(self(), "Hello World!")
"Hello World!"
```

send/2 gives us back the message as its return value, but that's not the same as retrieving the message from IEx's mailbox. We need receive/1 for that:

```
iex> receive do
...> msg -> "Here's the message: #{msg}"
...> after 100 -> "Nothing to see here."
...> end
"Here's the message: Hello World!"
```

receive/1 works a lot like case/2. We pattern match for messages on the left side of the arrow and define what to do with that message on the right. We're matching with a variable msg, so this will always match.

We added an after clause to avoid locking up IEx. receive/1 blocks until there is a message in the mailbox. If we had tried to run receive/1 without a message in the mailbox and without an after clause, it would have blocked forever, leaving us without an easy way to actually send a message and unblock it. The after clause releases receive/1 after the specified number of milliseconds, executing the code on the right side of the arrow.

If you ever do lock up IEx accidentally with receive/1, pressing Ctrl+C twice will still exit the session and get you back to the command prompt.

Long-Running Processes

To see how linking processes and trapping exits behave, we'll need processes that hang around long enough for us to observe them. IEx is a long-running process that is readily available, but we'll need to spawn others for it to interact with.

To do that, let's define a new module at lib/islands_engine/demo_proc.ex. All we'll need is a single function that implements an infinite recursion. We'll call ours loop/0. In the middle, we'll use receive/1 to retrieve the next message from the mailbox.

```
supervisor/lib/islands_engine/demo_proc.ex
defmodule IslandsEngine.DemoProc do
  def loop() do
    receive do
      message -> IO.puts "I got a message: #{message}"
    end
    loop()
  end
end
```

We don't need an after block here. This code will run in a separate process, so it will never block IEx. More importantly, though, we *want* this to block until there is a new message. It creates a little back pressure to keep this infinite recursion from just spinning and spinning.

With the DemoProc module in place, let's start a new IEx session and try this out:

```
iex> alias IslandsEngine.DemoProc
IslandsEngine.DemoProc

iex> self()
#PID<0.122.0>
```

Great; so we know what the IEx PID is. We'll check it again later to see whether or not it has changed.

Now let's use spawn/3 to spawn a new process, passing it the module DemoProc, the function :loop, and an empty list of arguments. We'll also bind the PID that spawn/3 returns to the spawned variable.

```
iex> spawned = spawn(DemoProc, :loop, [])
#PID<0.125.0>
```

To make sure we're working with a truly long-running process as we had hoped, we can check that the PID bound to the spawned variable points to a living process:

```
iex> Process.alive?(spawned)
true
```

We can also send this new process a message and check to make sure it receives it:

```
iex> send(spawned, "Hello World!")
I got a message: Hello World!
"Hello World!"
```

It does, and that all looks great. Now we're going to force that process to exit and see what happens:

```
iex> Process.exit(spawned, :kaboom)
true
```

Process.exit/2 takes the process to terminate as well as a reason for termination. The reason can be any Elixir term, but we'll just give it the atom :kaboom.

There are three categories of reasons for a process to terminate: :normal, :kill, and any other failure. A normal termination won't send an exit signal, so it won't terminate any other linked processes. :kill and any other reason will cause the process to send an exit signal.

```
iex> Process.alive?(spawned)
false
```

```
iex> self()
#PID<0.122.0>
```

```
iex> receive do
...> msg -> "Here's the message: #{msg}"
...> after 100 -> "Nothing to see here."
...> end
"Nothing to see here."
```

That process just vanished without a trace. The IEx process has the same PID that it did before, and the process we killed didn't send a message to IEx when it exited.

Recall that we want a supervising process to know if one of those processes should crash. Let's go fix that now.

Linking Processes

The way to get processes to know when other processes crash is to link them. That's what we'll explore next.

In the same IEx session, let's start by spawning a new process and have the IEx process link to it:

```
iex> linked = spawn(DemoProc, :loop, [])
#PID<0.128.0>
```

```
iex> Process.link(linked)
true
```

```
iex> Process.alive?(linked)
true
```

```
iex> send(linked, "Hello Process!")
I got a message: Hello Process!
"Hello Process!"
```

Use spawn_link to Avoid Race Conditions

When we spawn a process first, then link to it, there's a small window of time where either process might terminate before the link is complete.

Kernel.spawn_link/3 eliminates that race condition. It is like spawning a process and then linking, except that it's an atomic action. There's no time separation between spawning and linking.

Now that we've linked the two processes, let's force the linked one to exit:

```
iex> Process.exit(linked, :kaboom)
** (EXIT from #PID<0.122.0>) evaluator process exited with reason: :kaboom

Interactive Elixir (1.5.1) - press Ctrl+C to exit (type h() ENTER for help)
```

That was a little different from the last time. Looks like IEx—PID 122—crashed.

When one of a group of linked processes crashes, it sends an exit signal to all the other processes that it's linked to, and they will all crash as well.

On the other hand, we still have a session, so it looks like IEx restarted. Let's check its PID to be sure:

```
iex> self()
#PID<0.131.0>
```

That's a new PID, so it did restart. We've just seen process supervision in action. IEx crashed, and its supervisor restarted it without much fuss.

Trapping Exits

Despite the crash, we're closer to the goal. The next step is for IEx to handle the exit signal from a linked process without crashing. This is where trapping exits comes in, and it's what we'll take a look at next.

Since IEx restarted, it lost all of its history. We'll need to re-alias DemoProc before we get going:

```
iex> alias IslandsEngine.DemoProc
IslandsEngine.DemoProc

iex> self()
#PID<0.131.0>
```

Great! Now let's spawn a new process:

```
iex> linked2 = spawn(DemoProc, :loop, [])
#PID<0.133.0>
```

Then let's have the IEx process trap exits.

Process.flag/2 allows us to set values for predetermined keys for a given process's metadata. It returns the last value the key we're resetting had. Previously, :trap_exit was false, and that's what we get back:

```
iex> Process.flag(:trap_exit, true)
false
```

By default, when a process receives an exit signal with any reason other than :normal, the process exits and propagates that exit signal to any other process it is linked to.

When :trap_exit is set to true, the process converts exit signals to messages of the form {:EXIT, from, reason}, which the process can handle like any ordinary message.

Now let's go ahead and link the new process and force it to exit:

```
iex> Process.link(linked2)
true

iex> send(linked2, "Hello Process!")
I got a message: Hello Process!
"Hello Process!"

iex> Process.exit(linked2, :kaboom)
true

iex> Process.alive?(linked2)
false
```

So far, so good. Now let's check IEx's mailbox for the message:

```
iex> receive do
...> msg -> "Here's the message: #{inspect(msg)}"
...> after 100 -> "Nothing to see here."
...> end
"Here's the message: {:EXIT, #PID<0.233.0>, :kaboom}"

iex> self()
#PID<0.131.0>
```

That behaved exactly as we had expected. IEx converted the exit signal from linked2 into a regular message that it could handle without crashing.

Supervisors handle all this behind the scenes for us. By implementing a supervisor, we'll eliminate the need to manually trap exits and link to other processes, but it's useful to know what they're doing on our behalf.

Now that you have a good understanding of what supervisors are doing behind the scenes, let's start working with them directly.

Introducing the Supervisor Behaviour

Process supervision begins with the supervisor Behaviour. You'll get an overview of it in this section. Over the next few sections, you'll see how to customize supervisor processes. Then we'll build a supervisor to monitor all the game processes in Islands.

Like GenServer, supervisor is an Elixir Behaviour that wraps an OTP Behaviour. In this case, that is :supervisor. Also like GenServer, we can spawn new processes from supervisor modules. These supervisor processes will do all the starting, monitoring, restarting, and stopping of other processes within an application.

We call any process under supervision a child process of the supervisor. Child processes can be workers, like 'GenServer' processes, or other supervisor processes.

Since supervisors can supervise other supervisors, we can build tree structures of supervised processes. These supervision trees allow us to be specific about how we supervise processes. By specifying different startup options, we can tailor the way a supervisor behaves for a given type of process.

When we define a new supervisor module, we describe how we want it to supervise its children, what restart strategy to use, and specify under which circumstances the supervisor should restart the process.

We can also define some circumstances under which the supervisor itself should terminate and restart. Consider the case of a process that crashes continually and doesn't successfully restart. There's clearly something wrong that restarts aren't fixing, and we wouldn't want those restarts to continue indefinitely.

Supervisors allow us to configure the maximum allowable number of restarts over a given period of time with the :max_restarts and :max_seconds options. The default value for :max_restarts is 3, and the default value for :max_seconds is 5.

Restart strategies are a little more involved than restart thresholds. Let's take a closer look at them next.

Supervision Strategies

Processes often depend on one another to do their work. If a child process crashes, restarting just that one process might not stabilize the application. In the event of a crash, a supervisor needs to decide whether to restart just the one crashed process or other processes as well. If it needs to restart others, it must decide which ones. Supervisors depend on restart strategies to make those decisions.

We're going to look at all the available strategies, see how they work, and learn how to choose the right one for a given situation.

Each supervisor process can supervise a number of child processes. Those child processes might have different types of relationships with one another.

Sometimes all the child processes depend on one another, so if one of them crashes, the others will be invalid. Sometimes they are all completely independent, so if one crashes, the others will be fine.

Child processes all start in a temporal order. In some cases, each depends on the processes that spawned before it, so that if one crashes, all the processes that started after it will be invalid.

The pattern supervisors follow when starting child processes matters as well. Some supervisors will start a fixed number of child processes at once, when the application starts. Others will need to start and stop a variable number of child processes at runtime.

Islands falls into that second category. We'll be starting and stopping Game processes all the time.

All of these conditions have an impact on which strategy we choose. Let's take a closer look at the strategies next.

One for One

With the one-for-one strategy, if a single process terminates, the supervisor will restart just that one process. This is best if the group of supervised processes can work independently of one another—in other words, if restarting the one process will not upset the functioning of the whole group of processes.

Let's say we have one supervisor supervising three workers. Then one of those workers crashes. The supervisor will restart only that one worker.

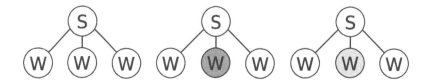

One for All

With the one-for-all strategy, if a single process terminates, the supervisor will terminate all the rest of the supervised processes and restart them all. This strategy is best if the group of processes do depend on each other, and each other's state, to work properly.

Imagine we have the same setup as before, and one worker crashes:

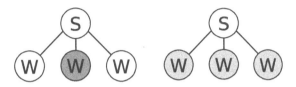

This time the supervisor will restart all the workers.

Rest for One

With the rest-for-one strategy, we need to look at a group of supervised processes as having a temporal order: the order they were started in. Let's assume that order goes from earliest to latest, left to right. If a process in the middle terminates, the supervisor will terminate all the processes that started after the problem process; then it will restart all the terminated processes. This strategy works best for groups of processes that have a temporal dependency—in other words, more newly spawned processes depend on the state and integrity of the processes started before them.

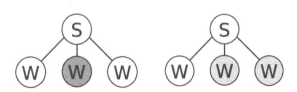

Simple One for One

The previous strategies are all fine, but they are not dynamic. They require the supervisor to start the new processes when we start the BEAM.

Islands is different; we'll be starting games and ending games all the time. For that, there's another strategy, simple one for one. This has a restart strategy similar to one-for-one. If an individual process terminates, the supervisor will restart just that one process.

The strategies are one way we can customize the way supervisors behave, but there are others. Let's take a look at another big piece of the puzzle next.

The Child Specification

The strategies describe a lot of how a supervisor will work with child processes, but they are not the whole story. There are a number of other options we can specify. Those options are stored in the child specification.

Fortunately, we don't have too much work to do here. The GenServer Behaviour creates a default child specification for us whenever we add the use GenServer line to a module. We can check the child spec for the Game module in IEx with child_spec/1, passing it the argument we want the supervisor to use as it starts a game.

```
iex> alias IslandsEngine.Game
IslandsEngine.Game

iex> Game.child_spec("Kusama")
%{id: IslandsEngine.Game,
  restart: :permanent,
  shutdown: 5000,
  start: {IslandsEngine.Game, :start_link, ["Kusama"]},
  type: :worker}
```

Let's run through these keys and see what they mean:

- :id is what the supervisor uses to identify each child specification.

- :restart tells the supervisor whether it should restart its child processes. :permanent means always restart the children. :temporary means never restart the children. And :transient means restart them only if they crash.

- :shutdown refers to the amount of time the supervisor should wait for the child process to shut down on its own before the supervisor actively kills it.

- :start is a three-element tuple that tells the supervisor which module, function, and arguments to use when starting or restarting child processes.

- :type is the type of child process the specification is for, either a worker or a supervisor.

With all that in mind, there are a couple of things we need to change about the default child specification for the Game module: the :start tuple, and the :restart type.

When we start games of Islands at runtime, we need to specify the name of the first player. We can't know that ahead of time, so we need to have the :start tuple reflect the fact that we can pass in any argument instead of specifying just one, as we did earlier.

Players will also need to stop game processes as well as start them. Otherwise, the BEAM wouldn't be able to reclaim the memory of completed game processes, and it would eventually crash. We'll need to specify the restart type as :transient.

We can generate a new child specification, passing in a keyword list of the new values we want, with Supervisor.child_spec/2. Let's take a look at how it works in IEx:

```
iex> spec = Supervisor.child_spec(Game, start: {Game, :start_link, []},
                                  restart: :transient)
%{id: IslandsEngine.Game,
  restart: :transient,
  shutdown: 5000,
  start: {IslandsEngine.Game, :start_link, []},
  type: :worker}
```

While Supervisor.child_spec/2 generates a new specification, it doesn't affect the existing Game module specification:

```
iex> Game.child_spec("Kusama")
%{id: IslandsEngine.Game,
  restart: :permanent,
  shutdown: 5000,
  start: {IslandsEngine.Game, :start_link, ["Kusama"]},
  type: :worker}
```

This is exactly the same as it was before. We can change the Game specification permanently by passing in the keyword list of new values into the use GenServer line in lib/islands_engine/game.ex:

```
use GenServer, start: {__MODULE__, :start_link, []}, restart: :transient
```

Let's recompile the Game module in IEx and check to make sure that the child specification reflects these changes:

```
iex> r Game
warning: redefining module IslandsEngine.Game
. . .
{:reloaded, IslandsEngine.Game, [IslandsEngine.Game]}

iex> Game.child_spec("Kusama")
%{id: IslandsEngine.Game,
  restart: :transient,
  shutdown: 5000,
  start: {IslandsEngine.Game, :start_link, []},
  type: :worker}
```

That's perfect. Notice that even though we passed the argument "Kusama" into Game.child_spec/1, because the function requires an argument, the child specification's :start tuple shows an empty list of arguments. That means that we can pass in any player's name at runtime and still start a new game.

We've done a lot of exploration and prep work. Time to build a supervisor for our game processes.

A Supervisor for the Game

Now that we have the Game module's child specification showing the values we want, we're ready to create a custom supervisor. We'll explore two ways to do this. One is as simple as starting a supervisor process with the right options. The other involves creating a new module that contains the callbacks we'll need as well as some helper functions we'll want.

Each game in Islands is a separate GenServer process. These processes will come and go as players start new games and then end them. We'll need a supervisor specifically to monitor games, and the :simple_one_for_one strategy is perfect for processes that we need to start and stop at runtime.

Most of the work of creating a custom supervisor comes in starting a new supervisor process with the right options. After that, the supervisor process itself does the rest. There are two ways to do this.

The most straightforward way is with the Supervisor.start_link/2 function. start_link/2 takes a list of child modules to start as well as a list of options. In our case, that would be the Game module and the :simple_one_for_one strategy.

We could also include new values for :max_restarts or :max_seconds in the list of options as well, but their default values are fine for our purposes.

The first thing that Supervisor.start_link/2 will do is get the child specification from any modules we specify. Because of that, we could pass in a list of child specifications instead, but we've already customized the specification for the Game module, so we can just pass in the module name.

Let's open up an IEx session to see how that works:

```
iex> alias IslandsEngine.Game
IslandsEngine.Game
```

```
iex> {:ok, sup} = Supervisor.start_link([Game], strategy: :simple_one_for_one)
{:ok, #PID<0.135.0>}
```

Now we have the PID of the supervisor process bound to the sup variable. We can use it to start any game processes we want, and they will all be supervised.

Supervisor.start_link/2 gets us going, but there is another approach we can take: creating a new module for our game supervisor. We'll be adding a couple of convenience functions for starting and stopping game processes, and a module will give us a convenient place to put them.

For this, we'll need to define a new GameSupervisor module at /lib/islands_engine/game_supervisor.ex. We'll bring in all the supervisor Behaviour code with use Supervisor. Let's go ahead and alias the Game module as well:

```
defmodule IslandsEngine.GameSupervisor do
  use Supervisor

  alias IslandsEngine.Game
end
```

Just as use GenServer created a child specification for us in the Game module, use Supervisor created one for the GameSupervisor module. We can see that specification with the child_spec/1 function.

```
iex> alias IslandsEngine.{Game, GameSupervisor}
[IslandsEngine.Game, IslandsEngine.GameSupervisor]
```

```
iex> GameSupervisor.child_spec(:any_argument)
%{id: IslandsEngine.GameSupervisor,
  restart: :permanent,
  start: {IslandsEngine.GameSupervisor, :start_link, [:any_argument]},
  type: :supervisor}
```

This is where we gain more control over the supervisor. If we needed to, we could pass in overrides to the child specification in the use Supervisor line just as we did for use GenServer in the Game module. We can also add public functions to this module for starting and stopping child processes. We'll do that a little later in the chapter.

Supervisor is a Behaviour, so we'll follow the same pattern we used for GenServer, adding a public function that wraps a module function that triggers a callback.

We can see from the :start tuple in the child specification that the GameSupervisor says that it will have a :start_link function to start a new supervisor process with.

Let's start there.

supervisor/lib/islands_engine/game_supervisor.ex
```
def start_link(_options), do:
  Supervisor.start_link(__MODULE__, :ok, name: __MODULE__)
```

start_link/1 wraps Supervisor.start_link/3, which is different from the Supervisor.start_link/2 that we used at the beginning of this section. It's much closer to the GenServer.start_link/3 we've used before.

We'll use the local name name: __MODULE__, ensuring that there can be only one supervisor process for this module. This also makes it possible to reference that process by the name of the module instead of the PID.

Supervisor.start_link/3 triggers the init/1 callback function. The main thing init/1 has to do is initialize the new supervisor process with Supervisor.init/2.

supervisor/lib/islands_engine/game_supervisor.ex
```
def init(:ok), do:
  Supervisor.init([Game], strategy: :simple_one_for_one)
```

Supervisor.init/2 works a lot like Supervisor.start_link/2. It takes a list of the kinds of processes we want it to supervise as well as a strategy.

Now that we have a GameSupervisor, we need to make sure it's started whenever we start up the BEAM so it will be available whenever we need it.

Starting the Supervision Tree

Supervisor processes can do their job only if they are running. We can't know in advance when a player is going to start a new game, so we need to make sure that the GameSupervisor is running as soon as the application starts up. That's what we'll focus on in this section.

We mentioned that since supervisors can supervise both workers and other supervisors, they can form trees of supervised processes. This implies that there is a single process at the root of the tree, and that the root node begins the process of starting the whole tree.

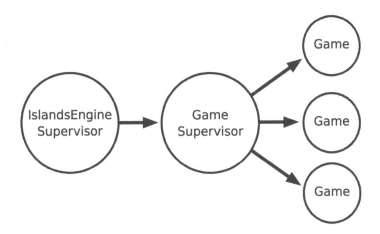

Back in Chapter 2, *Model Data and Behavior*, on page 9, when we generated the islands_engine project, we passed in the --sup flag to mix new. That automatically created an application.ex file for us, and the start/2 function in that file starts a top-level supervisor process called IslandsEngine.Supervisor.

```
def start(_type, _args) do
  children = [
    {Registry, keys: :unique, name: Registry.Game}
  ]

  opts = [strategy: :one_for_one, name: IslandsEngine.Supervisor]
  Supervisor.start_link(children, opts)
end
```

Currently, that supervisor process starts the Registry as a worker, but we'll also have it start a new GameSupervisor process whenever we start the application. We'll use that GameSupervisor process to start and supervise each new game.

To do that, we just need to add IslandsEngine.GameSupervisor to the list of children, and IslandsEngine.Supervisor will start it when we start the application.

```
children = [
  {Registry, keys: :unique, name: Registry.Game},
  IslandsEngine.GameSupervisor
]
```

That's great. We can start a new GameSupervisor process when the application starts, so it will be available as players want to start new games. Now we need to have that process start worker processes, which is to say games of Islands.

Starting and Stopping Child Processes

We want each new game to be supervised. That means that we need the GameSupervisor process to start them. As the GameSupervisor process starts new game processes, under the hood it will link to them and trap exits so that it can receive ordinary messages if any of the games should crash.

Let's start by adding a public start_game/1 function in the GameSupervisor module to start games with. Once we have the supervisor starting the processes, it will take care of the rest for us.

supervisor/lib/islands_engine/game_supervisor.ex
```
def start_game(name), do:
  Supervisor.start_child(__MODULE__, [name])
```

Here's what happens when we call start_game/1:

- __MODULE__ here evaluates to GameSupervisor, which is the local name we gave the supervisor process. The supervisor Behaviour will translate this into the supervisor process PID.

- GameSupervisor looks up the child_spec for the Game module, which is the type of child we told it to start in GameSupervisor.init/1, Supervisor.init([Game], strategy: :simple_one_for_one).

- The Game module's child_spec tells the supervisor to use the Game module and the start_link/1 function to start the child.

- GameSupervisor passes in the argument we supplied name to Game.start_link/1 to start and supervise the game.

And with that, the players can have fun playing the game.

Once the game is over, we don't want idle game processes hanging around in the BEAM using memory. We need a programmatic way of stopping games when they're over.

Let's add a stop_game/1 function to GameSupervisor. We'll have it take the first player's name, just as start_game/1 does:

```
def stop_game(name) do
  Supervisor.terminate_child(__MODULE__, pid_from_name(name))
end
```

Supervisor.terminate_child/2 does the real work of stopping the process, but it expects to receive both the supervisor module and the PID to stop.

We will need a new pid_from_name/1 function to find the actual PID with the player's name:

supervisor/lib/islands_engine/game_supervisor.ex
```
defp pid_from_name(name) do
  name
  |> Game.via_tuple()
  |> GenServer.whereis()
end
```

Let's take these functions out for a spin in IEx.

After we alias the Game and GameSupervisor, we can start a game with start_game/1:

```
iex> alias IslandsEngine.{Game, GameSupervisor}
[IslandsEngine.Game, IslandsEngine.GameSupervisor]

iex> {:ok, game} = GameSupervisor.start_game("Cassatt")
{:ok, #PID<0.119.0>}
```

Great—we got a new game. Now let's get a via tuple that we'll use in a minute.

```
iex> via = Game.via_tuple("Cassatt")
{:via, Registry, {Registry.Game, "Cassatt"}}
```

While we're here, Supervisor gives us a couple of useful functions. count_children/1 takes a supervisor module and returns a map describing all the child processes for it:

```
iex> Supervisor.count_children(GameSupervisor)
%{active: 1, specs: 1, supervisors: 0, workers: 1}
```

which_children/1 also takes a supervisor module and returns a list of tuples describing each child process under supervision:

```
iex> Supervisor.which_children(GameSupervisor)
[{:undefined, #PID<0.119.0>, :worker, [IslandsEngine.Game]}]
```

Now let's call stop_game/1 and check to make sure that the GameSupervisor kills the original PID but doesn't restart a new one:

```
iex> GameSupervisor.stop_game("Cassatt")
:ok

iex> Process.alive?(game)
false

iex> GenServer.whereis(via)
nil
```

That's just what we wanted. Not only is the original game process no longer alive, but there is no other process registered with the via tuple either.

There's another case we need to handle before we're done with this section. What happens if a player starts a game and then abandons it somewhere along the way? We don't want to let those processes just sit there taking up system resources.

Fortunately, GenServer gives us an automated way to have processes time out and shut themselves down if they haven't received a new message in a given number of milliseconds. All we need to do is add a fourth element to any of the GenServer reply tuples: a positive integer representing the number of milliseconds to wait before timing out {:reply, :some_reply, %{}, 1000}.

Let's add some modifications to the Game module so that game processes will time themselves out when they're inactive. First, let's set a module attribute to fifteen seconds—long enough to write quick commands in IEx, but short enough to wait for:

```
@timeout 15000
```

Then let's add it to the return tuple for Game.init/1:

```
def init(name) do
. . .
  {:ok, %{player1: player1, player2: player2, rules: %Rules{}}, @timeout}
end
```

We also wrote the reply_success/2 function in the Game for handling all successful replies from the server process. Let's add the timeout value to the end of that reply tuple as well:

```
defp reply_success(state_data, reply) do
  {:reply, reply, state_data, @timeout}
end
```

For the sake of completeness, you could add timeout to all the error clauses. Alternately, you could create a reply_error/2 function to handle errors and refactor all the error tuples in the Game module to use it.

When a GenServer process times out, it will receive a :timeout message. In order to really stop the GenServer, though, we need to handle that message and return a :stop tuple. We can do that with a new clause of handle_info/2.

```
supervisor/lib/islands_engine/game.ex
def handle_info(:timeout, state_data) do
  {:stop, {:shutdown, :timeout}, state_data}
end
```

Tagging the return tuple with :stop causes the Behaviour to trigger the terminate/2 callback. GenServer provides a default implementation of terminate/2 for us, so we should be all set.

With the timeouts set, let's start a new game, check to see whether the game process is alive, and then wait a little while and check again:

```
iex> alias IslandsEngine.{Game, GameSupervisor}
[IslandsEngine.Game, IslandsEngine.GameSupervisor]

iex> {:ok, game} = GameSupervisor.start_game("Cassatt")
{:ok, #PID<0.130.0>}

iex> Process.alive?(game)
true

iex> Process.alive?(game)
false
```

That's perfect. The game starts up fine but times out after fifteen seconds—just as we wanted it to.

In order to keep game processes from timing out prematurely while we're working on the rest of the book, go ahead and set the @timeout value to some high value, like a day's worth of milliseconds:

```
@timeout 60 * 60 * 24 * 1000
```

We're in a good place. We've got a GameSupervisor process started as part of the whole supervision tree. We've also got functions to start and stop games that make them a part of this supervision tree as well.

It's time to see how all of this work we've done so far behaves in the console.

Putting the Pieces Together

Now that we have all the pieces assembled, let's see how they all work together in IEx. We can start by aliasing the Game and GameSupervisor modules:

```
iex> alias IslandsEngine.{Game, GameSupervisor}
[IslandsEngine.Game, IslandsEngine.GameSupervisor]
```

Now we can use the GameSupervisor.start_game/1 function to start a new game:

```
iex> {:ok, game} = GameSupervisor.start_game("Hopper")
{:ok, #PID<0.119.0>}
```

Note that the PID is number 119. If we generate a via tuple for the first player's name and check its PID with GenServer.whereis/1, it should be the same:

```
iex> via = Game.via_tuple("Hopper")
{:via, Registry, {Registry.Game, "Hopper"}}
```

```
iex> GenServer.whereis(via)
#PID<0.119.0>
```

Great—we do get the same PID.

Now let's add a second player and check the game process's state to make sure we've got both players' names:

```
iex> Game.add_player(via, "Hockney")
:ok
```

```
iex> state_data = :sys.get_state(via)
. . .
```

```
iex> state_data.player1.name
"Hopper"
```

```
iex> state_data.player2.name
"Hockney"
```

Good—they're both set.

Now let's force the game to exit and see what happens:

```
iex> Process.exit(game, :kaboom)
true
```

```
iex> GenServer.whereis(via)
#PID<0.128.0>
```

The first thing we see is that the via tuple points to a different PID. This tells us a couple of things. Not only did the the supervisor restart the process after the exit, but the Registry noticed and reset the new PID to the old key. That's pretty nice.

Now let's check the state to see which players' names we have set:

```
iex> state_data = :sys.get_state(via)
. . .
```

```
iex> state_data.player1.name
"Hopper"
```

```
iex> state_data.player2.name
nil
```

Interesting. The first player's name is still correct, but we don't have the second player's name at all.

The supervisor remembered the original argument we started the game with, the first player's name, but that's it. The rest of the state is gone. In some cases, this is just fine. For Islands, though, losing state toward the end of a long game would be really frustrating.

In the next section, you'll learn how to hang on to that state and restore it if a process happens to exit abnormally.

Recovering State After a Crash

This is where we really fulfill the promise of fault tolerance. It's one thing to restart a process if it crashes and then move on. It's another thing entirely to restart it and restore the last known good state.

The way we'll do this is to save a copy of the data outside of the current process, or any other process the current one is linked to. We'll do this when we initialize the process, and then again whenever the state changes.

Whenever we start a new process, or restart a crashed process, we'll check for that saved state. If it exists, that means we're restarting, so we'll use the saved version. If it doesn't exist, that means it's a new process, so we'll use fresh state.

The storage engine we'll use is ETS, which is short for Erlang Term Storage. ETS comes with OTP, and it allows us to store data in in-memory tables as two-element tuples. The first element of each tuple is the key; the second is the value.

ETS tables offer a number of different options to choose from to specify how they store data and which processes can access it.

There are four different types of ETS tables: :set, :ordered_set, :bag, :duplicate_bag. :set is the default type.

- :set tables store exactly one value per key.

- :ordered_set tables behave the same as :set tables, except that they order the keys.

- :bag tables store multiple values under the same key, as long as the values are not exact duplicates.

- :duplicate_bag tables store multiple values under the same key, even if they are exact duplicates.

There are three levels of privacy: :private, :protected, and :public. :protected is the default.

- :private means that only the process that started the table can read to or write from it.

- :protected means that the process that started the table can read from and write to the table. All other processes can only read from it.

- :public means that all processes can read from and write to the table.

There is also the :named_table option, which allows us to reference that table by the name instead of needing to keep track of a reference to it.

Getting Started with ETS

In order to start using ETS, we need to create a new table with the Erlang :ets.new/2 function. :ets.new/2 takes an atom for the name of the table we're creating as well as a list of options. Once we have a new table, we'll see how the CRUD operations work—creating, retrieving, updating, and deleting records.

Let's try this out with a test example. We'll make a public set table named :test_table. Since :set is the default table type, we don't need to include it in the list of options.

```
iex> :ets.new(:test_table, [:public, :named_table])
:test_table
```

We can insert values into the table with :ets.insert/2, which takes the table name and a two-element tuple with both the key and the value:

```
iex> :ets.insert(:test_table, {:key, "value"})
true
```

We can retrieve values with :ets.lookup/2, which takes the table name and the key we want the value for:

```
iex> :ets.lookup(:test_table, :key)
[key: "value"]
```

This returns a keyword list containing both the key and the value.

:ets.insert/2 will overwrite any existing value for the key. If we call it with the same key and a different value, it will store only the new value:

```
iex> :ets.insert(:test_table, {:key, "new value"})
true

iex> :ets.lookup(:test_table, :key)
[key: "new value"]
```

If we try to look up a key that doesn't exist, we'll get an empty list in return:

```
iex> :ets.lookup(:test_table, :wrong_key)
[]
```

We can also delete a key and its value with :ets.delete/2, passing it the table name and the key to delete:

```
iex> :ets.delete(:test_table, :key)
true

iex> :ets.lookup(:test_table, :key)
[]
```

That gets us through the basics of ETS. We're ready to use it to solve our data recovery problem.

Step one is to make sure we have a table available whenever IslandsEngine is running. We'll need it to be public so that all game processes will have read and write access. It should be a set so that we can have only one game state per key. Let's call the table :game_state.

We can make the table available by adding a call to :ets.new/2 in the start/2 function in lib/islands_engine/application.ex:

```
def start(_type, _args) do
. . .
    :ets.new(:game_state, [:public, :named_table])
    opts = [strategy: :one_for_one, name: IslandsEngine.Supervisor]
    Supervisor.start_link(children, opts)
  end
end
```

Now that we'll have a table available at runtime, we need to make sure to store game state and retrieve it when we need to.

Storing and Retrieving Game State

We'll want to store the full state for each game in the :game_state table whenever it changes. We register each game process by the name of the first player, so that name makes a great key to store the state under.

For game processes, some state will change whenever there is a successful reply—either in the game itself or in the state machine data. Luckily, we wrote a single function in the Game module to handle successful replies: reply_success/2. A call to :ets.insert/2 with the name of :player1 as the key and the full game state as the value is all we need.

supervisor/lib/islands_engine/game.ex
```
defp reply_success(state_data, reply) do
  :ets.insert(:game_state, {state_data.player1.name, state_data})
  {:reply, reply, state_data, @timeout}
end
```

Any time we start or restart a process, GenServer will trigger the init/1 callback. That makes init/1 a good place to check the :game_state table for any state stored under the first player's name.

If :ets.lookup/2 returns an empty list, we generate fresh state the way init/1 had done before. If :ets.lookup/2 returns some state, we'll use that instead.

We can add a new private function that returns the state of a new game given the first player's name:

supervisor/lib/islands_engine/game.ex
```
defp fresh_state(name) do
  player1 = %{name: name, board: Board.new(), guesses: Guesses.new()}
  player2 = %{name: nil,  board: Board.new(), guesses: Guesses.new()}
  %{player1: player1, player2: player2, rules: %Rules{}}
end
```

Then we can use that new function in init/1:

```
def init(name) do
  state_data =
  case :ets.lookup(:game_state, name) do
    [] -> fresh_state(name)
    [{_key, state}] -> state
  end

  :ets.insert(:game_state, {name, state_data})
  {:ok, state_data, @timeout}
end
```

This will work for Islands because the ETS lookup is quite fast. But init/1 blocks while it is evaluating. If the lookup happened to take a long time, this would block the GameSupervisor.start_game/1 function until init/1 returned. In a really busy system, that could cause problems.

We can fix this by having the process send a message to itself inside init/1 asking to set the state:

supervisor/lib/islands_engine/game.ex
```
def init(name) do
  send(self(), {:set_state, name})
  {:ok, fresh_state(name)}
end
```

This will let init/1 return immediately, and the {:set_state, name} message will appear in the new process's mailbox.

Moot @timeout

 We should remove the @timeout from the return tuple in init/1 because the game process will always receive a new message immediately from send(self(), {:set_state, name}). This makes it impossible for the process to ever time out.

In GenServers, the callback for handling regular messages is handle_info/2, so let's define a new clause that matches that message. Then we can move all the state checking and setting logic into this new handle_info/2 clause:

```
supervisor/lib/islands_engine/game.ex
def handle_info({:set_state, name}, _state_data) do
  state_data =
  case :ets.lookup(:game_state, name) do
    [] -> fresh_state(name)
    [{_key, state}] -> state
  end
  :ets.insert(:game_state, {name, state_data})
  {:noreply, state_data, @timeout}
end
```

That should handle it.

We removed the @timeout from the return tuple of init/1, but we put it back here. This is now the last callback to return from the initial call to start_link/1. There won't automatically be a new message in the game process's mailbox right after this, so the timeout will be able to do its job.

While this works, it does introduce a race condition. It's important to understand why we have a race condition and talk about the code we've written that mitigates the risk.

We register game processes by name with the Registry. Other processes can send messages to them with a :via tuple at any time—whether the PID exists or not, and whether the state is properly reset after a crash or not. This means it's possible for another message to get in front of our :set_state message during a restart. In Islands, this risk is low because of the small number of messages sent to any single game.

The state machine offers a level of protection here as well. When init/1 returns, it sets fresh state in the game, which means that the state is :initialized. The only action we can take in that state is adding another player. Any other action will return an error, effectively ignoring that message and bringing the :set_state message to the top, or one step closer to the top, of the game's mailbox. This is not an ironclad guarantee, but we have minimized the potential for harm.

Let's take this new code out for a spin in IEx and see if it behaves the way we want it to. We'll alias the Game and GameSupervisor modules, and then start a new game:

```
iex> alias IslandsEngine.{Game, GameSupervisor}
[IslandsEngine.Game, IslandsEngine.GameSupervisor]

iex> {:ok, game} = GameSupervisor.start_game("Morandi")
{:ok, #PID<0.130.0>}
```

Let's look up the game state for the "Morandi" key. The first player should have a name, but the second player shouldn't:

```
iex> [{"Morandi", value}] = :ets.lookup(:game_state, "Morandi")
. . .

iex> value.player1.name
"Morandi"

iex> value.player2.name
nil
```

Nice—exactly what we expected to see.

Now let's add a second player and check the state in the :game_state table. If everything worked correctly, both players should have names set this time:

```
iex> Game.add_player(game, "Rothko")
:ok

iex> [{"Morandi", value}] = :ets.lookup(:game_state, "Morandi")
. . .

iex> value.player1.name
"Morandi"

iex> value.player2.name
"Rothko"
```

That's perfect.

Now for the moment of truth. Let's force the game process to exit. That will kill the process for the PID bound to the game variable. Generating a via tuple will get us back to the new process the supervisor restarted for us. We can check its state with :sys.get_state/1, and if this all worked, both players will have the correct names.

```
iex> Process.exit(game, :kaboom)
true
```

```
iex> via = Game.via_tuple("Morandi")
{:via, Registry, {Registry.Game, "Morandi"}}

iex> state_data = :sys.get_state(via)
. . .

iex> state_data.player1.name
"Morandi"

iex> state_data.player2.name
"Rothko"
```

That's fantastic—just what we were looking for.

We're almost done; all we have left is some housekeeping to take care of when a process exits.

Cleaning Up After a Game

We're saving the state of each game in the :game_state table, but so far, we haven't removed that state when the game is over. :game_state will continue to grow and use memory unless we delete a game's key from the :game_state table when the supervisor terminates the child process, or when the child process times out.

In order to clean that data up when a game ends normally, we'll add a call to :ets.delete/2 in the GameSupervisor.stop_game/1 function.

supervisor/lib/islands_engine/game_supervisor.ex
```
def stop_game(name) do
  :ets.delete(:game_state, name)
  Supervisor.terminate_child(__MODULE__, pid_from_name(name))
end
```

Cleaning up the data after a GenServer timeout is a little more involved, but not much. One of the callbacks the GenServer Behaviour defines is terminate/2. This is the proper place to do any cleanup before the process exits, and it's where the call to :ets.delete/2 should go.

The wrinkle is that we shouldn't call :ets.delete/2 every time a game process terminates, but only when it times out. If a process crashes, we still want to keep the data.

We've already got a clause of handle_info/2 that handles the :timeout message and returns a tagged :stop tuple.

Tagging the return tuple with :stop causes the Behaviour to trigger the terminate/2 callback. It will pass the middle term of the return tuple in as the first argument so we can pattern match on it.

We'll need a terminate/2 clause that matches {:shutdown, :timeout}. In it, we'll call :ets.delete/2 to clean up the game state. Then we'll create a catchall clause to handle any other kind of exit.

supervisor/lib/islands_engine/game.ex
```
def terminate({:shutdown, :timeout}, state_data) do
  :ets.delete(:game_state, state_data.player1.name)
  :ok
end
def terminate(_reason, _state), do: :ok
```

All either clause of terminate/2 needs to return is :ok.

Let's see how this works in the console. We'll start by aliasing the modules we'll need and then starting a game:

```
iex> alias IslandsEngine.{Game, GameSupervisor}
[IslandsEngine.Game, IslandsEngine.GameSupervisor]

iex> {:ok, game} = GameSupervisor.start_game("Agnes")
:ok, #PID<0.119.0>}
```

Let's check to make sure that the via tuple for this game matches the PID of the game we just started:

```
iex> via = Game.via_tuple("Agnes")
{:via, Registry, {Registry.Game, "Agnes"}}

iex> GenServer.whereis(via)
:ok, #PID<0.119.0>}
```

Then let's stop the game and check to make sure that the game process is no longer alive:

```
iex> GameSupervisor.stop_game("Agnes")
:ok

iex> Process.alive? game
false
```

Now we can make sure that the GameSupervisor didn't start a new process, and that there is no lingering data in the :game_state table:

```
iex> GenServer.whereis(via)
nil

iex> :ets.lookup(:game_state, "Agnes")
[]
```

That's exactly what we expected to see.

What we have so far will let us recover from almost anything, but there's a little more work we can do. ETS is an in-memory data store. What happens when the BEAM's memory goes away? What happens when the host reboots? We'll answer those questions next.

Data Durability

The code we've written so far will work great as long as the BEAM stays up. If we restart the BEAM for any reason, though, the ETS table we created will be gone along with all its data. To handle BEAM restarts, we need more durability.

The way to get that durability looks a lot like the way we're recovering data from ETS, just taken one step further. To recover state when a process restarts, we store it outside of the process, or any processes linked to it. To recover state after a BEAM restart, we need to store the state outside the BEAM.

The shape of the code we currently have will work for this. All the functions are in place and working the way we want them to. We'll just need to swap out ETS for another storage mechanism.

This is where the number of available options grows enormously. There's no way to cover them all in a single section of this chapter. What we can do is look at some OTP options as well as a strategy that will apply broadly to a lot of other options.

OTP offers two options right off the bat. DETS is a disk-based version of ETS.[1] DETS starts tables with :dets.open_file/2 instead of :ets.new/2, but the query API is remarkably similar to ETS. This is the durable option with the least change to the existing code.

Mnesia is OTP's distributed database management system. It's considerably more complex to set up and use than ETS or DETS. While it is likely to be overkill for the needs of a game like Islands, it might be a great fit for other applications you might be working on. Take a look at the documentation if you're interested.[2]

Stepping outside of OTP, a single broad strategy will work with a large number of data stores. The idea is to convert the game state to JSON. Once the data is in JSON, the data storage world is our oyster. We can store the game state as a JSON data type practically anywhere.

With any of these strategies, the game state will be stored safely out of the BEAM in case the node goes down for any reason. Using the functions and callbacks that we've already set up, we'll query for it, and set it back in each process's state.

---

1. http://erlang.org/doc/man/dets.html
2. http://erlang.org/doc/apps/mnesia/Mnesia_chap1.html

Wrapping Up

What we've done in this chapter is really pretty remarkable. We started with game processes that could crash and lose all their state at any time. We've ended up with games that will recover from any crash and restore their state to the last good version, automatically.

Try that in any other language.

Along the way, we've explored linking processes and trapping exits. We've looked at ways to customize the way supervisors behave with restart strategies and child specifications. We've also seen how to start and stop supervised processes. As a bonus, we've gotten an introduction to ETS as well.

We're headed into Part 3 of the book next. That's where we'll layer on a Phoenix interface and make Islands available on the web.

Part III

Add a Web Interface with Phoenix

Now that we have our game engine, it's time to provide a way to interact with that logic via the web. Phoenix does a fabulous job at this. We'll be generating a fresh Phoenix application and pulling in our game engine as a dependency. Since our game engine maintains state, we are in an ideal situation to make use of the persistent, multiplexed connections that Phoenix channels provide.

Let's get to it!

What we'll do in this chapter

- *generate a new Phoenix application—without Ecto*
- *bring in our game engine as a dependency*
- *incorporate our game engine in the web interface's super-vision tree*

CHAPTER 6

Generate a New Web Interface with Phoenix

Phoenix is a great web framework. It's fast, really fast. Its components are familiar and easy to work with. Phoenix is lightweight, modular, and explicit. There's almost no hidden magic. That's a big boost for maintainability.

Frameworks are nearly ubiquitous in web development today. For either the front end or back end, almost everyone uses some form of framework to build web applications.

There's good reason for this. Frameworks get us up and running quickly. They remove the need to reimplement common tasks for every project—routing, handling request parameters, and the like. Frameworks let us focus on our individual application's behavior instead of repetitive tasks.

The slippery slope is that frameworks make it all too easy to tangle the framework components and the application together in ways that really hurt us.

Elixir Applications let us get around this in an elegant way. Phoenix itself is an Application. The game engine we built in Parts 1 and 2 of the book is also an Application.

Our task in Part 3 of this book is to create a web interface with Phoenix for our game. We're going to use the Phoenix and game engine Applications as building blocks to create a third Application that will keep the Phoenix interface separate from the game in a way that will make our job trivially easy.

Frameworks

Framework components represent what is common to all web applications. That's why the framework creators extracted them out into the framework.

This is a great boon to developers because we don't need to solve the same problems over and over again. Things like routing requests to the right handler functions, getting the request parameters, handling response templates, setting cookies—the framework takes care of all that for us. The framework components make it easy to interact with the business logic over the web. They make up the web interface for the application.

The business logic is unique to each application. This is the part that we can't extract into a common framework. It's what makes our application do interesting things and gives it value. It's the most important part to us, because the success or failure of our application depends on how well this works.

But there's a serious, hidden-in-plain-sight problem here. We're so accustomed to it that we hardly even notice.

Coupling

The way we normally build business logic with a framework is completely backward. We create application behavior by adding more pieces of the framework—routes, controllers, models, and views. Each new model or controller we add contains a bit more logic. This mixes our business domain with the domain of the framework, and it couples the two inextricably and forever.

Why is that a big deal? We can't easily reuse the business logic with another interface. We can't test our business logic in isolation, outside the context of the framework code.

Let's say we wanted both a web interface and a Nerves device version of Islands. If we didn't have a separate Application for Islands, we would need to completely reimplement the business logic for each interface.

Whenever we need to send an HTTP request to test a business rule, an alarm should go off at our workstation. Business rules should be completely separate from how we handle HTTP requests. Yet this is how we've been trained to test web applications.

This is why upgrading a framework to a new major version can sometimes be so painful. It's also why switching frameworks entirely seems like a herculean task. The way we normally work with frameworks makes this pain almost inevitable.

Which brings us to one of the most important points in the entire book.

Phoenix Is Not Your Application

It's important to think about how we got into this situation, so we know how to get out of it.

The way we talk about web applications gets us in trouble right away. We say, "I'm building a Rails app" or an Ember app or a Phoenix app or an Elm app.

But that's not true. What we're really doing is building a chat app, or a banking app, or a game called Islands, with a Phoenix interface or an Ember interface or an Elm interface.

The problem is deeper than that, though. There are a number of ways to look at it, but this resonates most with me. ORMs lead us directly into this coupling of business logic and framework components.

ActiveRecord models in Rails offer the clearest example of this, but the same idea applies across many frameworks. Let's say we are working in a domain in which one of the entities is a bicycle. We could begin modeling this with a plain Ruby class:

```
class Bicycle
  # We define bicycle-specific properties and behavior here.
end
```

We might define bicycle properties here like wheels, handlebars, pedals, and brakes. We could also define behaviors like pedaling, steering, and braking.

Rails tends to push us toward putting domain models, like our Bicycle class, in a database. ActiveRecord makes this very easy. We just have a model class inherit from ActiveRecord::Base:

```
class Bicycle < ActiveRecord::Base
  # Suddenly, bicycle behavior is mixed with database behavior.
end
```

With this small change, everything is different. Our Bicycle class suddenly knows a lot more than just bicycle things. It knows how to connect to a database, read from and write to a table, validate data, perform transactions, generate queries, and a whole host of other things.

Our domain, in which a bicycle is just a bicycle, is suddenly entwined with the Rails domain, in which a Bicycle model is an interface to a database table. Once this happens, the two domains become glued together and can't be separated without a rewrite.

Decoupling

That's not going to happen here. We already have our game logic separated out. Now we're going to layer on the web interface. The two will live happily side by side, and they won't be tightly coupled.

We built the core logic of the game as an Application. That means we can bring it into any other Application as a dependency, and all of its functionality will be available to us. Phoenix happens to be an Application, which makes this job a snap. This one idea, this way of managing dependencies and building applications, is quietly revolutionary. It's going to make the rest of our work with Phoenix seem trivial.

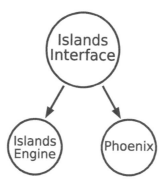

Of course, Erlang developers have been working in this quietly revolutionary way for a couple of decades now.

All our core logic needs is a web interface, and we'll use Phoenix to build one. Phoenix has all of the MVC components you're used to for those times when HTTP's request/response cycle fits best. It's also got a real-time, persistent connection layer called channels built right in.

This is where all our hard work up to now is going to really pay off. From here, we'll be able to generate a fresh Phoenix project and bring our whole game in as a dependency. As we build out the interface, we won't be mixing in any application logic. We'll just call into the public interface of the game server that we've already built. There won't be any entanglement between the game and the interface.

Applications are what allow us to build these separate, self-contained components. They're what allow us to compose them back together into larger applications as well. We'll explore them next.

Applications

Despite the name, Applications are not what we normally think of as software applications. They are reusable units of code that are bigger than modules. In fact, they most often contain multiple modules. They're similar in scale to libraries in other ecosystems. While they can function as libraries, they can also be so much more.

Applications can act as true building blocks for our programs, a means of putting together integral pieces of business logic to build a larger whole. Working with larger building blocks like these makes us really productive.

Applications can also stand on their own as what we traditionally think of as an application. The IslandsEngine Application we developed in the first part of the book is one example. It is a fully functioning game just as it is, albeit with a pretty unfriendly user interface. As complete as it is, we can still use it as a building block for something larger, as we'll soon see.

:application is a specific OTP Behaviour written in Erlang, just like :gen_server. There is a module in OTP that defines :application-specific functions as well as a list of callbacks we need to implement. Elixir provides a wrapper module around the pure Erlang one called Application. We'll be using the Elixir wrapper most often in this chapter.

The Application Behaviour lets us do three things. It lets us define and name Applications. It facilitates dependency management among Applications. We can define hierarchies of Application dependencies, and the Behaviour will make sure they work correctly. The Behaviour also facilitates cleanly starting and stopping individual applications in a running BEAM.

"Cleanly" here means two things. It makes sure to start any dependent Applications before it starts itself. It also keeps track of any processes the Application spawns during startup or while it's running, and makes sure to stop them when the Application stops.

Now that we've got an idea of the significance of Applications, let's dig a little deeper and see how they work.

Understanding Applications

The good news is that we've been working with an Application all along. At the beginning of the book, when we generated the brand-new IslandsEngine project, Mix automatically created it as an Application. We didn't need to look deeply at the Application Behaviour then because IslandsEngine stood on its own for our purposes.

Now, though, we need to use it as a dependency, as a building block to create a larger project—the web interface we're going to build in this chapter. Understanding Application dependencies will clarify our work on this project, and any other Elixir projects we work on.

We already have examples of the Application Behaviour–related files in IslandsEngine. We'll use them to understand dependency management as well as starting and stopping individual applications inside the BEAM. We'll see firsthand the independence of Applications that lets us solve the coupling problem so prevalent in web applications.

There are three parts to the implementation of an Application, and Mix has a hand in all of them.

When we generate a project with mix new we get a file named mix.exs at the root of our project. mix.exs defines key aspects of the Application, everything from its name and version number to a list of applications it depends on to build the project.

Mix also generates a Behaviour callback module in the /lib directory that is named after our project. In the case of our game engine, it generated /lib/islands_engine/application.ex. If we supply the --sup flag to mix new, the callback module will contain the start/2 callback function necessary to start the top-level supervisor for the Application. Without --sup, the file will be there, but it will be empty.

Once we compile the project, mix will generate an application resource file, written in Erlang, that the BEAM will use to work with our Application.

Let's take a look at these files now starting with mix.exs.

Managing Dependencies

Any project's mix.exs file has two main functions—defining a project's metadata and managing its dependencies. Of the two, dependency management is by far the most common thing developers do, and it's the most important for our purposes as well.

Three functions defined in mix.exs do all the work for us. The project/0 function returns a keyword list of metadata about the application.

```
def project do
  [
    app: :islands_engine,
    version: "0.1.0",
    elixir: "~> 1.5",
    start_permanent: Mix.env == :prod,
    deps: deps()
  ]
end
```

The app name, version number, and Elixir version are pretty self-explanatory. start_permanent: starts the system in such a way that the BEAM will crash if the top-level supervisor crashes. This will be true for the production environment as well.

The deps: key holds a list of build-time dependencies this application depends on. The value here is the return value of the deps/0 function, also defined in mix.exs.

```
defp deps do
  []
end
```

IslandsEngine has no dependencies, so the return value here is an empty list. When we generate a new Phoenix project in the next section, we'll see an example with a number of dependencies.

There are actually two types of dependencies for Applications: those that matter for runtime, and those that come into play for build/compile time. Mix uses the dependencies listed in the deps/0 function to build the project. Any Application in this list can have its own dependencies. This is how we can compose a larger tree of dependencies, just as we saw with supervision trees in Chapter 5, *Process Supervision for Recovery*, on page 97.

The last function in mix.exs is application/0. It returns a keyword list of data related to starting the application. The value of the :extra_applications key is a list of application names, which are the runtime dependencies. Mix will make sure these are running before it starts :islands_engine. :mod holds a tuple for the module name of the callback module as well as a list of options that the start/2 function in that module might need.

```
def application do
  [extra_applications: [:logger],
    mod: {IslandsEngine.Application, []}]
end
```

IslandsEngine depends only on the :logger Application at runtime. This dependency is a default for all Applications Mix generates. Elixir itself supplies this, so we don't need to list it in the deps/0 function.

The reason that there are two different places to define dependencies is that it's possible to need a dependency for compilation but not need it to be running inside the BEAM, and vice versa.

If our Application doesn't have a supervision tree—for example, if we omitted the --sup flag when we generated the project—we can omit the mod key completely:

```
def application do
  [extra_applications: [:logger]]
end
```

You might be thinking that this seems a little redundant. Shouldn't Mix be able to infer the Application list from the deps list as long as we give it some clues? As of Mix 1.4, it can.

If the runtime dependencies are the same as the compile-time ones, we can omit the :extra_applications key in application/0:

```
def application do
  [mod: {IslandsEngine.Application, []}]
end
```

If there are runtime dependencies not listed in the deps/0 function—:logger, for instance—we can handle that with the :extra_applications key:

```
def application do
  [extra_applications: [:logger],
   mod: {IslandsEngine.Application, []}]
end
```

And if we have compile-time dependencies that we don't need to start when we start our application, we can mark them as runtime: false in the deps/0 function:

```
defp deps do
  [{:some_new_dep, "> 0.0.0", runtime: false}]
end
```

That brings us to the end of dependency management in mix.exs. Once we have defined the dependencies, we need to be able to start them inside the BEAM. That's where we're headed next.

Starting and Stopping Applications

Applications are so independent, we can start and stop them individually in the BEAM. When we start an individual Application, OTP will start any necessary supervisor or worker processes along with it. When we stop that same Application, OTP makes sure to stop those supervisors and workers as well.

The work of defining which processes to start all comes together in the callbacks file. In the IslandsEngine project, that's /lib/islands_engine/application.ex.

Back in Chapter 5, *Process Supervision for Recovery*, on page 97, we took a good look at this file in the context of supervision trees. We won't need to go over it in much detail, but we should point out the use Application line that makes this module an Application Behaviour.

We should also quickly mention the start/2 function, which is there to start the top-level supervisor for the Application. Along the way, it's going to make sure that any child processes—supervisors or workers—get started as well.

```elixir
defmodule IslandsEngine.Application do
  @moduledoc false

  use Application

  def start(_type, _args) do
    children = [
      {Registry, keys: :unique, name: Registry.Game},
      IslandsEngine.GameSupervisor)
    ]

    :ets.new(:game_state, [:public, :named_table])
    opts = [strategy: :one_for_one, name: IslandsEngine.Supervisor]
    Supervisor.start_link(children, opts)
  end
end
```

When we compile the project, Mix takes information from mix.exs and produces an application resource file, like this one at /_build/dev/lib/islands_engine/ebin/islands_engine.app.

This will always live in the /_build/dev/lib/<application_name>/ebin/ directory and be named after our Application, with an .app file extension.

The contents of this file are what the BEAM needs in order to properly handle our Application.

```erlang
{application,islands_engine,
            [{applications,[kernel,stdlib,elixir,logger]},
             {description,"islands_engine"},
             {modules,['Elixir.IslandsEngine',
                       'Elixir.IslandsEngine.Application',
                       'Elixir.IslandsEngine.Board',
                       'Elixir.IslandsEngine.Coordinate',
                       'Elixir.IslandsEngine.Game',
```

```
                      'Elixir.IslandsEngine.GameSupervisor',
                      'Elixir.IslandsEngine.Guesses',
                      'Elixir.IslandsEngine.Island',
                      'Elixir.IslandsEngine.Rules']},
          {registered,[]},
          {vsn,"0.1.0"},
          {extra_applications,[logger]},
          {mod,{'Elixir.IslandsEngine.Application',[]}}]}.
```

Now that we've taken a good look at all the pieces, let's take this out for a spin to see if we can learn more about how it behaves.

If you've ever wondered why running iex at the root of a project doesn't load that project and start the applications but running iex -S mix does, you're about to see why.

The -S flag tells IEx to run a script before opening the shell. Notice that mix.exs has the .exs file extension, signifying that it's a script file. The mix part is short for mix run, which will run a given script in the context of an Application. The default script to run is mix.exs.

Running mix.exs triggers the Behaviour callback function start/2 that we just saw in the callback module. That will start our Application as well as any Applications it depends on.

Let's go ahead and start a plain iex session from the root of our islands_engine project. This will be a generic IEx session that will not start :islands_engine.

:application exposes a handy function called which_applications/0 that will show us which Applications are currently running. This function isn't defined on Elixir's Application wrapper module, so we call it on the Erlang module instead. Let's see what it tells us:

```
iex> :application.which_applications
[{:logger, 'logger', '1.5.1'}, {:iex, 'iex', '1.5.1'},
 {:elixir, 'elixir', '1.5.1'}, {:compiler, 'ERTS  CXC 138 10', '7.1'},
 {:stdlib, 'ERTS  CXC 138 10', '3.4'}, {:kernel, 'ERTS  CXC 138 10', '5.3'}]
```

Each running Application shows up as a three-tuple. Among the others, Elixir itself is an Application. This is pretty much the bare minimum for running an IEx session.

Now let's quit out of that session and start a new one with iex -S mix, and then run :application.which_applications/0 again:

```
iex> :application.which_applications
[{:islands_engine, 'islands_engine', '0.1.0'}, {:logger, 'logger', '1.5.1'},
 {:mix, 'mix', '1.5.1'}, {:iex, 'iex', '1.5.1'}, {:elixir, 'elixir', '1.5.1'},
 {:compiler, 'ERTS  CXC 138 10', '7.1'}, {:stdlib, 'ERTS  CXC 138 10', '3.4'},
 {:kernel, 'ERTS  CXC 138 10', '5.3'}]
```

Great—now we see our :islands_engine Application, and we also see :mix itself, since we implicitly invoked mix run.

If we start a new IEx session without starting the Application—like this: iex -S mix run --no-start—we'll see that the :islands_engine Application isn't running but :mix still is:

```
iex> :application.which_applications
[{:logger, 'logger', '1.5.1'}, {:mix, 'mix', '1.5.1'}, {:iex, 'iex', '1.5.1'},
 {:elixir, 'elixir', '1.5.1'}, {:compiler, 'ERTS  CXC 138 10', '7.1'},
 {:stdlib, 'ERTS  CXC 138 10', '3.4'}, {:kernel, 'ERTS  CXC 138 10', '5.3'}]
```

We can start :islands_engine manually with Application.start(:islands_engine):

```
iex> Application.start(:islands_engine)
:ok
```

```
iex> :application.which_applications
[{:islands_engine, 'islands_engine', '0.1.0'}, {:logger, 'logger', '1.5.1'},
 {:mix, 'mix', '1.5.1'}, {:iex, 'iex', '1.5.1'}, {:elixir, 'elixir', '1.5.1'},
 {:compiler, 'ERTS  CXC 138 10', '7.1'}, {:stdlib, 'ERTS  CXC 138 10', '3.4'},
 {:kernel, 'ERTS  CXC 138 10', '5.3'}]
```

If we try to start it again, we get an error saying that it's already started:

```
iex> :application.start(:islands_engine)
{:error, {:already_started, :islands_engine}}
```

We can also stop it with Application.stop(:islands_engine):

```
iex> Application.stop(:islands_engine)
:ok

20:55:42.291 [info]  Application islands_engine exited: :stopped
nil
```

```
iex> :application.which_applications
[{:logger, 'logger', '1.5.1'}, {:mix, 'mix', '1.5.1'}, {:iex, 'iex', '1.5.1'},
 {:elixir, 'elixir', '1.5.1'}, {:compiler, 'ERTS  CXC 138 10', '7.1'},
 {:stdlib, 'ERTS  CXC 138 10', '3.4'}, {:kernel, 'ERTS  CXC 138 10', '5.3'}]
```

Now let's see the Application Behaviour's runtime dependency management in action. While :islands_engine is stopped, let's also stop :logger, and then try to restart :islands_engine:

```
iex> :application.stop(:logger)
:ok

iex>
=INFO REPORT==== 20-Jan-2017::21:32:08 ===
    application: logger
    exited: stopped
    type: temporary
nil
```

```
iex> :application.which_applications
[{:mix, 'mix', '1.5.1'}, {:iex, 'iex', '1.5.1'}, {:elixir, 'elixir', '1.5.1'},
 {:compiler, 'ERTS  CXC 138 10', '7.1'}, {:stdlib, 'ERTS  CXC 138 10', '3.4'},
 {:kernel, 'ERTS  CXC 138 10', '5.3'}]
iex> :application.start(:islands_engine)
{:error, {:not_started, :logger}}
```

The Behaviour correctly remembered that :islands_engine depends on :logger and wouldn't start :islands_engine because :logger wasn't running.

:application exposes another handy function, ensure_all_started/1, which will behave the same as start/2, making sure all the runtime dependencies are running before trying to start the Application we pass in.

```
iex> :application.ensure_all_started(:islands_engine)
{:ok, [:logger, :islands_engine]}
```

```
iex> :application.which_applications
[{:islands_engine, 'islands_engine', '0.1.0'}, {:logger, 'logger', '1.5.1'},
 {:mix, 'mix', '1.5.1'}, {:iex, 'iex', '1.5.1'}, {:elixir, 'elixir', '1.5.1'},
 {:compiler, 'ERTS  CXC 138 10', '7.1'}, {:stdlib, 'ERTS  CXC 138 10', '3.4'},
 {:kernel, 'ERTS  CXC 138 10', '5.3'}]
```

That's great. It's exactly what we expected to see.

Now that we've seen how Applications work, we're ready to generate a new Phoenix project and bring IslandsEngine in as a dependency.

Generate a New Phoenix Application

This is where the fun really begins. With just a couple of shell commands we'll have a new web app up and serving pages, and Phoenix will serve them faster than you might have thought possible.

Before we start, make sure you have the Phoenix installer archive as well as Node.js installed on your system. Take a look at Appendix 1, *Installing System Dependencies*, on page 189 if you need help installing them. Node.js is only necessary to manage front-end dependencies, including Brunch, which Phoenix uses as a build tool. Node.js doesn't play a role within Phoenix proper.

By default, the Phoenix project generator will install Ecto, the Elixir data wrapping and query generating package. The generator will also install Brunch by default.

We won't need to use Ecto because we won't be using a database. We will use Brunch, though, because we'll need to serve some assets for the web version of our game.

We will call the Phoenix interface project islands_interface. We will pass that name into the phx.new Mix task that the installer archive exposes as well as the --no-ecto flag telling phx.new not to install Ecto.

Let's change out of the the islands_engine into its parent directory. That way, when we run the phx.new task, we'll create the interface directory parallel to the engine directory.

```
$ mix phx.new islands_interface --no-ecto
* creating islands_interface/config/config.exs
. . . # Creating lots more files here
* creating islands_interface/web/views/page_view.ex
```

Once the project generator is done creating files, it will ask if we want to install the application dependencies. We should say yes by either typing a "y" or just pressing Return.

```
Fetch and install dependencies? [Yn] y
* running mix deps.get
* running npm install && node node_modules/brunch/bin/brunch build
```

Before we move on, let's take a quick look at the functions in mix.exs that the project generator created. We'll start with the project/0:

```
def project do
  [app: :islands_interface,
   version: "0.0.1",
   elixir: "~> 1.3",
   elixirc_paths: elixirc_paths(Mix.env),
   compilers: [:phoenix, :gettext] ++ Mix.compilers,
   build_embedded: Mix.env == :prod,
   start_permanent: Mix.env == :prod,
   deps: deps()]
end
```

The most important thing to notice here is the name of our Application. It's :islands_interface, not :phoenix. The project generator didn't create a "Phoenix Application"—it created a new Application for us with its own identity, above Phoenix itself.

The deps/0 function tells us more:

```
defp deps do
  [{:phoenix, "~> 1.2.1"},
   {:phoenix_pubsub, "~> 1.0"},
   {:phoenix_html, "~> 2.6"},
   {:phoenix_live_reload, "~> 1.0", only: :dev},
   {:gettext, "~> 0.11"},
   {:cowboy, "~> 1.0"}]
end
```

Our :islands_interface Application brings in :phoenix, the Application, as well as other Phoenix-related Applications as dependencies. :islands_interface is the root node of a tree of dependencies, and these others are the next layer of nodes down.

The application/0 function doesn't hold any surprises. It makes sure that we start all the dependencies listed in deps/0:

```
def application do
  [
    mod: {IslandsInterface.Application, []},
    extra_applications: [:logger, :runtime_tools]
  ]
end
```

Okay, let's get back to the installation process. After Mix fetched all our project's dependencies, it told us what our next steps should be:

```
We are all set! Run your Phoenix application:

    $ cd islands_interface
    $ mix phx.server

You can also run your app inside IEx (Interactive Elixir) as:

    $ iex -S mix phx.server
```

Let's follow those directions now. Change into the project directory and start the server with mix phx.server:

```
$ cd islands_interface/
$ mix phx.server
==> fs (compile)
Compiled src/sys/inotifywait_win32.erl

. . . # Lots of compilation here

==> islands_interface
Compiling 11 files (.ex)
Generated islands_interface app
[info] Running IslandsInterface.Endpoint with Cowboy using http on port 4000
22 Jul 09:12:05 - info: compiled 5 files into 2 files, copied 3 in 1.2 sec
```

By executing mix phx.server, we trigger the initial compilation of all the Elixir files in the project. That will generate the application resource file at /_build/dev/lib/islands_interface/ebin/islands_interface.app.

You might also see a warning about a new hex version that's available. Feel free to follow the instructions for upgrading.

```
A new Hex version is available (0.12.1), please update with `mix local.hex`
```

Now for the really exciting part. The very last bit of the compilation message lets us know that the Erlang web server Cowboy is running our app on port 4000. Let's point a web browser at http://localhost:4000 and see what we get.

Just for fun, go ahead and reload the welcome screen a few times and take a look at the terminal screen that you started the Application from.

```
[info] GET /
[debug] Processing by IslandsInterface.PageController.index/2
  Parameters: %{}
  Pipelines: [:browser]
[info] Sent 200 in 263µs
[info] GET /
[debug] Processing by IslandsInterface.PageController.index/2
  Parameters: %{}
  Pipelines: [:browser]
[info] Sent 200 in 224µs
[info] GET /
[debug] Processing by IslandsInterface.PageController.index/2
  Parameters: %{}
  Pipelines: [:browser]
[info] Sent 200 in 186µs
[info] GET /
[debug] Processing by IslandsInterface.PageController.index/2
  Parameters: %{}
  Pipelines: [:browser]
[info] Sent 200 in 197µs
```

Yes, with Phoenix, we can measure the page load times in *microseconds.*

We're ready to perform the quietly revolutionary act we talked about at the beginning of this chapter. We're going to bring in the logic for Islands as both a build-time and runtime dependency for our new application.

Adding a New Dependency

Now that we have a new Application to act as the web interface, we need to bring the game engine in as a dependency. The interface needs to have access to all the game logic we wrote in the first two parts of the book. In particular, it must be able to see all the public functions in the IslandsEngine.Game module.

This works just like any other dependency in Elixir, and it is about as easy as it can possibly be. Only two steps are involved.

We'll need to compile IslandsEngine in with the rest of the project as well as start it when we start the IslandsInterface Application.

To make :islands_engine a compile-time dependency, we'll add it to the deps/0 function in islands_interface/mix.exs:

```
defp deps do
  [
    {:phoenix, "~> 1.3.0"},
    {:phoenix_pubsub, "~> 1.0"},
    {:phoenix_html, "~> 2.10"},
    {:phoenix_live_reload, "~> 1.0", only: :dev},
    {:gettext, "~> 0.11"},
    {:cowboy, "~> 1.0"},
    {:islands_engine, path: "../islands_engine"}
  ]
end
```

Notice that we used a path dependency for :islands_engine. That allows us to provide the pathname to a project on the local filesystem, and the Elixir package manager, Hex, will take care of the rest. That's it. We can give this a try in the console by running iex -S mix phx.server at the root of the islands_interface project.

The first thing we should do is see which Applications are running with :application.which_applications/0:

```
iex> :application.which_applications()
[{:islands_interface, 'islands_interface', '0.0.1'},
 {:phoenix_live_reload, 'Provides live-reload functionality for Phoenix',
  '1.1.3'},
 {:file_system,
  'A file system change watcher wrapper based on
    [fs](https://github.com/synrc/fs)',
  '0.2.2'},
```

```
{:phoenix_html,
 'Phoenix.HTML functions for working with HTML strings and templates',
 '2.10.5'}, {:cowboy, 'Small, fast, modular HTTP server.', '1.1.2'},
{:cowlib, 'Support library for manipulating Web protocols.', '1.0.2'},
{:ranch, 'Socket acceptor pool for TCP protocols.', '1.3.2'},
{:islands_engine, 'islands_engine', '0.1.0'},
{:runtime_tools, 'RUNTIME_TOOLS', '1.12'}, {:logger, 'logger', '1.5.1'},
{:gettext, 'Internationalization and localization through gettext', '0.13.1'},
{:phoenix,
 'Productive. Reliable. Fast. A productive web framework that
  does not compromise speed and maintainability.\n',
 '1.3.0'},
{:phoenix_pubsub, 'Distributed PubSub and Presence platform\n', '1.0.2'},
{:eex, 'eex', '1.5.1'},
{:poison, 'An incredibly fast, pure Elixir JSON library', '3.1.0'},
{:plug,
 'A specification and conveniences for composable modules between
  web applications',
 '1.4.3'}, {:mime, 'A MIME type module for Elixir', '1.1.0'},
{:hex, 'hex', '0.15.0'}, {:inets, 'INETS  CXC 138 49', '6.4'},
{:ssl, 'Erlang/OTP SSL application', '8.2'},
{:public_key, 'Public key infrastructure', '1.4.1'},
{:asn1, 'The Erlang ASN1 compiler version 5.0', '5.0'},
{:crypto, 'CRYPTO', '4.0'}, {:mix, 'mix', '1.5.1'}, {:iex, 'iex', '1.5.1'},
{:elixir, 'elixir', '1.5.1'}, {:compiler, 'ERTS  CXC 138 10', '7.1'},
{:stdlib, 'ERTS  CXC 138 10', '3.4'}, {:kernel, 'ERTS  CXC 138 10', '5.3'}]
```

That's a lot more Applications running than we had with :islands_engine. The main things to note are that both :islands_engine and :islands_interface started. Also note that Phoenix itself is listed as a started Application.

Since both the :islands_engine and :islands_interface Applications are available, let's see if we can start a new game from the console using the public interface of IslandsEngine.Game:

```
iex> IslandsEngine.Game.start_link("Betty")
{:ok, #PID<0.465.0>}
```

That's perfect. We can start up a new game from within the Phoenix interface. Once we have the game's PID, we can use it to call any of the public IslandsEngine.Game functions.

With :application.which_applications/0 we can see which applications are running at any given time, but we don't get a sense of the structure—the tree of Applications and their dependencies.

Mix gives us a tool to do this: the deps.tree task. Let's run it at the root of the islands_interface project:

```
$ mix deps.tree
islands_interface
├── gettext ~> 0.11 (Hex package)
├── islands_engine (../../new_islands)
├── phoenix_pubsub ~> 1.0 (Hex package)
├── cowboy ~> 1.0 (Hex package)
│   ├── cowlib ~> 1.0.2 (Hex package)
│   └── ranch ~> 1.3.2 (Hex package)
├── phoenix_html ~> 2.10 (Hex package)
│   └── plug ~> 1.0 (Hex package)
│       ├── cowboy ~> 1.0.1 or ~> 1.1 (Hex package)
│       └── mime ~> 1.0 (Hex package)
├── phoenix ~> 1.3.0 (Hex package)
│   ├── cowboy ~> 1.0 (Hex package)
│   ├── phoenix_pubsub ~> 1.0 (Hex package)
│   ├── plug ~> 1.3.3 or ~> 1.4 (Hex package)
│   └── poison ~> 2.2 or ~> 3.0 (Hex package)
└── phoenix_live_reload ~> 1.0 (Hex package)
    ├── file_system ~> 0.2.1 or ~> 0.3 (Hex package)
    └── phoenix ~> 1.0 or ~> 1.2 or ~> 1.3 (Hex package))
```

This confirms what we suspected, that :islands_interface is at the root of this tree. The important thing to notice is that both :islands_engine and :phoenix are parallel and equal in this tree. Both live *under* :islands_interface, and both provide functionality to make the whole web application work.

This is a subtle but critical point. It's what allows us to let the interface talk to the game logic's public interface, and keeps the two nicely decoupled. That's the theory. Now let's prove it.

Call the Logic from the Interface

We've seen that we can start a new game from within an IEx session begun with iex -S mix phx.server. That means we can call the public functions of the IslandsEngine.Game module from any Phoenix component.

At the beginning of this chapter, we talked a lot about decoupling the interface from the business logic. We made a bold claim and said that this would make our work trivially easy. Throughout the chapter, we've shown how we can keep the two separated but included in a common project. What we haven't yet shown is how those two will communicate. It's time to back up that claim.

We're going to walk through this pretty quickly. We'll be working with a few new files, but we won't be spending a lot of time explaining them.

The good news is that Phoenix provides a full, working example of all the files we'll need. It's the welcome page we saw when we started the server for the first time. We're going to modify some of those files to perform an experiment.

The first thing we'll do is create a form in the index template /islands_interface/web/templates/page/index.html.eex. We'll use the form_tag/2 and tag/2 functions from the :phoenix_html Application. You'll recall that we saw :phoenix_html in our list of dependencies from mix.exs.

```
<div class="jumbotron">
  <h2><%= gettext "Welcome to %{name}", name: "Phoenix!" %></h2>
  <p class="lead">
    A productive web framework that does not compromise speed and
    maintainability.
  </p>
  <p>
    <%= form_tag("/test") do
      [tag(:input, type: "text", name: "name"),
       tag(:input, type: "submit", value: "New Game")]
    end%>
  </p>
</div>
```

With form_tag/2, the default action is POST, and we pass it the route /test. The tag/2 functions create a text input for a player's name and a submit button.

We just told that form to post all requests to /test, which is a route we don't currently have. Let's add it now in islands_interface/web/router.ex:

```
scope "/", IslandsInterface do
  pipe_through :browser # Use the default browser stack

  get "/", PageController, :index
  post "/test", PageController, :test
end
```

That route says that any POST request to /test should be handled by the test function in the IslandsInterface.PageController module. That module exists, but the function doesn't, so let's add it now to islands_interface/web/controllers/page_controller.ex:

```
defmodule IslandsInterface.PageController do
  use IslandsInterface.Web, :controller

  alias IslandsEngine.GameSupervisor

  def index(conn, _params) do
    render conn, "index.html"
  end

  def test(conn, %{"name" => name}) do
    {:ok, _pid} = GameSupervisor.start_game(name)
    conn
    |> put_flash(:info, "You entered the name: " <> name)
    |> render("index.html")
  end
end
```

In the function head, we pattern match on %{"name" => name}. This second argument is the incoming parameters map from the request. The match binds the value of the "name" key to the name variable, and makes it available inside the body of the test function.

Notice that we're pattern matching for a successful start of the game server {:ok, _pid} = GameSupervisor.start_game(name). If the game server fails to start, we'll get an error page.

We're also setting a flash message that will let us know which name we entered into the form, and then we're re-rendering the same index page we were just on.

Go ahead and start the server from the root of the IslandsInterface project with $ iex -S mix phx.server. Then head over to http://localhost:4000/ with your favorite browser. The form we just put in the index.html.eex file should now be there.

Before we do anything, let's make sure that the game supervisor hasn't started any games yet:

```
iex> alias IslandsEngine.GameSupervisor
IslandsEngine.GameSupervisor

iex> Supervisor.which_children(GameSupervisor)
[]
```

Now go ahead and add a name to the input field and hit submit. That should take you right back to the welcome page, and you should see the name you entered at the top of the page in a flash message.

At this point, you can go back to the terminal window to check for the POST request you should have gotten by submitting the form:

```
iex> [info] POST /test
[debug] Processing by IslandsInterface.PageController.test/2
  Parameters: %{"_csrf_token" => "<long_string_omitted>",
                "_utf8" => "✓", "name" => "Frank"}
  Pipelines: [:browser]
[info] Sent 200 in 55ms
```

Great—that looks like just what we want.

Let's check that the game supervisor actually started a new game process:

```
iex> Supervisor.which_children(GameSupervisor)
[{:undefined, #PID<0.361.0>, :worker, [IslandsEngine.Game]}]
```

And we can see that it did. Excellent.

For fun, try entering exactly the same name into the form and hitting submit again. You should get an error page telling you that the game server was already started as shown in the figure on page 152. Recall that we registered each game server with a name based on the string we pass in to start the game, and we can start only one server at a time with that name.

That's exactly the error we get.

Now that we can start a game server, and we know that the IslandsEngine.Game module is available inside Phoenix components in IslandsInterface, the world is our oyster. We can call any of the game server's public functions from any module in IslandsInterface. This is what will allow us to play Islands on the web.

Wrapping Up

We've done a lot in this chapter in a short amount of time. We created a new project for our web interface. We brought the game logic in as a dependency, and we got the interface to call into the game server.

That's the surface-level view. Looking at it more deeply, we've solved one of the most vexing problems related to using web frameworks. We've created a clean separation between logic and interface that will make testing and maintaining our application a breeze. If we ever need to upgrade to a newer major version of Phoenix, it'll be a much, much easier task than it would be with other frameworks.

At this point, we're ready to tackle one of the most exciting parts of Phoenix—channels. Channels provide persistent, stateful connections between stateful back ends and front ends, and they scale beautifully. That's where we're headed next.

What we'll do in this chapter

- *create a channel that communicates directly with a GenServer*
- *use the topic:subtopic convention to focus communication on a single GenServer*
- *define separate handle_in events for each game command— new game, join game, fire shot, and so on*
- *interact with our channel in the console to see it work*

CHAPTER 7

Create Persistent Connections with Phoenix Channels

Phoenix channels are just amazing. They really are Phoenix's killer feature. They provide persistent connections between stateful servers and stateful clients. They're incredibly fast, and they can truly scale.

Channels allow us to fulfill the promise we made in the very beginning of this book: to connect a stateful back end to a stateful front end with a persistent, stateful connection.

We're going to build a channel that will allow us to directly interact with the game engine. The channel callback functions we define will match the public interface of the game. We'll build new functionality with callbacks in our own new channel module, and then we'll exercise those callbacks in two browser window consoles to mimic two players playing the game.

The Beauty of Channels

Channels fundamentally change the nature of what we are able to do on the web.

Channels scale incredibly well. In one test on a powerful machine, the Phoenix team was able to establish two million simultaneous channel connections. These weren't just static connections. The team was able to broadcast messages to all two million clients within a few seconds.

Let that sink in for a minute. Think about what your application would look like if every user of your system had her own persistent connection to the server.

Channels are soft-real-time communication conduits. Clients join a channel on a specific topic. That's the same as saying that clients subscribe to a topic on a channel. Then they're able to facilitate conversations on those topics. Channels are multiplexed, so a single channel can support bidirectional messages on many topics.

Most often, the client is a front-end web client, but it could be anything that knows how to send a message to a channel, including another server.

It's tempting to think of channels as equivalent to raw WebSockets, the most common protocol that channels use for transporting data. The reality is that channels offer a lot of nice features over WebSockets alone. Channels can transport data over a number of different protocols, including custom ones you can write yourself. By default, they'll use WebSockets, and fall back to long polling if WebSockets aren't available.

Channels also handle failure well. When networks lose connection, channels know how to reestablish communication and carry on where they left off. That's the kind of thing you need to build yourself if you're using WebSockets alone.

Channels require less code to implement than traditional MVC components. There's a single module to write callbacks in instead of a controller, view, template, and schema.

The key to our game channel implementation is that there will be no business logic in the channel. All the channel callbacks will simply call directly into the game engine, pattern match on the response, and determine the correct reply to send back to the client.

Another way to look at this is that the channel will be concerned only with the behavior that is appropriate for this layer—determining which response to reply with and figuring out which clients to send that response to.

Before we move on to implementing our own channel, let's take a look at the moving parts that make up a channel.

The Pieces That Make a Channel

We often talk about Phoenix channels as if each one is a single, monolithic entity that works on its own. In fact, there are a number of moving parts acting in harmony across multiple layers that make channels work as well as they do.

Let's take a quick look at the most important ones to get a better feeling for the whole.

The Channel Module

The channel module is the tip of the iceberg, the visible part that we will interact with the most. It's a custom Behaviour defined within Phoenix. The Behaviour specifies that we define a join/3 callback for allowing clients to join a specific topic as well as multiple handle_in/3 callbacks to match, handle, and respond to messages sent from clients.

Socket

Phoenix.Socket is also a custom Behaviour defined in the Phoenix application. It is responsible for establishing and maintaining the connection between clients and a channel. The socket also keeps track of which transport method the channel uses.

Socket is also a struct used to define and hold the state of the connection. It's analogous to the connection struct in the stateless MVC parts of Phoenix.

Transport

Channels rely on protocols to move messages between the client and the server. That's what the transport layer is for. Phoenix ships with two types of transports built in: WebSockets and long polling.

Socket.Transport is also an API for building transports. It's possible to create your own custom transport layer for whatever protocol you like by following the Socket.Transport API.

Phoenix PubSub

Channels are very flexible in the way they allow us to route messages from the channel to clients. That's handled by a separate package called phoenix_pubsub. PubSub is short for "publish and subscribe," and it's a way for clients to register with a channel (subscribe) in order to get sent published messages. The way clients subscribe is via the join/3 callback function.

Presence

Phoenix Presence is an incredible piece of technology. It uses data types from cutting-edge computer science research—conflict-free replicated data types (CRDTs)—in a web framework you can use right now.

Presence solves the hardest and most extreme edge cases in keeping track of clients in channels—multiple nodes in a distributed cluster, clients connected on multiple devices, and anything going wrong with either the network or the clients. Presence solves these problems in a mathematically provable way.

Not only does Presence solve the original problem of channel membership, it also promises to be useful for service discovery, process discovery, and anything that we need to track on BEAM nodes distributed across a network.

Client Code

Channels on the server are only half the story. We need clients to complete the picture. Channel client packages exist for a number of different languages and platforms. We'll use the JavaScript client that ships with Phoenix as we write functions directly in a browser window's JavaScript console.

That's the lay of the land. We've got all the info we need to get started, so we might as well dive right in. We're going to implement the channel as well as the JavaScript necessary for the front end to talk to it.

Let's Build It

The big picture for this final chapter is that we're opening up the public interface we created for the game server to the web. The game server is a stateful system. Modern web front ends are also stateful. We're going to build a Phoenix channel as a stateful, persistent connection between these two stateful systems. This new channel's public interface will become the mechanism clients will use to interact with the game.

Here's the Plan

We're going to build that channel function by function, and we'll check its behavior at each step along the way by calling JavaScript code in the browser's developer tools console. We want the new channel to communicate directly with an individual GenServer process for a game. Since channels multiplex messages, a single channel can handle clients sending messages to many topics—which is to say that a single channel can handle the communication for many games. Checking that this communication works means that we'll need to be able to see what's happening from the browser all the way down to the server.

To fully exercise this, we're going to use two separate browser windows. That will mimic two players playing the game on the web. We'll work with the developer tools JavaScript console in each browser window. We'll also have an IEx session open to check what's happening to the state of the game server.

That setup is going to look like the figure on page 157.

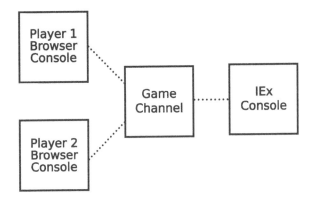

There are a lot of moving parts here, and at times it might seem like building a model ship in a bottle. I'm going to err on the side of clarity over brevity to make this easier to follow.

To help with clarity, let's stick with a convention. We'll keep the two browser windows open side by side, and we'll say that the window on the left represents player1, and the window on the right is player2.

Go ahead and run iex -S mix phx.server at the root of the islands_interface project.

Then open up two browser windows and go to localhost:4000 in each. Once you're there, open up the developer tools console in each window. For Chrome, they're under the View menu, View -> Developer -> Developer Tools. When the developer tools pane opens up, click on the Console link.

That should look like this:

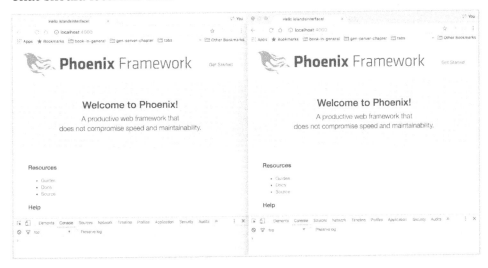

With the server started, we already have a stateful back end running. The good news is that we won't have to build out a full front-end application to exercise this. Your favorite browser's JavaScript engine is a fine stateful front-end environment to work with. The browser's developer tools console will let us run code directly in that environment.

Here's the plan for how we'll work for the rest of the chapter. We'll write some code in a new channel module and recompile it in the IEx session. Then we'll go into the JavaScript console, push some messages down the channel to exercise that code, and then check in the IEx console to see what happened. We'll follow that pattern for each new piece of functionality we build.

Define a New Module

The first thing we need is a channel module. Let's get one started at lib/islands_interface_web/channels/game_channel.ex:

```
channel/lib/islands_interface_web/game_channel.ex
defmodule IslandsInterfaceWeb.GameChannel do
  use IslandsInterfaceWeb, :channel

  alias IslandsEngine.{Game, GameSupervisor}
```

In order to make it behave like a channel, we use IslandsInterfaceWeb :channel. That triggers the existing channel/0 function in the IslandsInterfaceWeb module, located at lib/islands_interface_web/islands_interface_web.ex:

```
def channel do
  quote do
    use Phoenix.Channel
    import IslandsInterfaceWeb.Gettext
  end
end
```

We'll also be working with the Game and GameSupervisor modules, so we need to alias them here.

With the proto-channel module in place, there are two pieces of housekeeping that we need to check in on: routing requests to our socket, and registering our channel with a socket.

The "route" to our socket appears in our project's endpoint at lib/islands_interface_web/endpoint.ex. Phoenix generated this for us when it created our project.

```
defmodule IslandsInterfaceWeb.Endpoint do
  use Phoenix.Endpoint, otp_app: :islands_interface

  socket "/socket", IslandsInterface.UserSocket
  . . .
```

The next step is to define a socket so we can establish a connection to the channel. Phoenix generated one for us already at web/channels/user_socket.ex. All we need to do is register our new game channel there:

```
defmodule IslandsInterface.UserSocket do
  use Phoenix.Socket

  channel "game:*", IslandsInterfaceWeb.GameChannel
```

The meaning here is that we want any messages with a topic that begins with "game:" to go through the GameChannel.

There's one more interesting piece to look at in IslandsInterface.UserSocket: the connect/2 function. Whenever a client attempts to connect to the socket, the request will make its way through the connect/2 function Phoenix defined for us:

```
def connect(_params, socket) do
  {:ok, socket}
end
```

This is a great spot to do any authentication work, or to assign any values to the socket so that they will pass through the system into the channel. For our purposes, we'll just pass right through by returning {:ok, socket}. We'll see the client side of this in action later.

With that configuration housekeeping out of the way, we're ready to start doing more with our game channel. We'll start with letting clients subscribe to it.

Join a Channel

Before clients can do anything more meaningful in a channel, they need to join it on a topic-subtopic combination. To let users do that, we need to implement a join/3 function in the IslandsInterfaceWeb.GameChannel module.

For now, we'll do the simplest thing we can and just let anybody join. We do that by just returning {:ok, socket}. We'll see how to get a little more picky about letting players join a little later on.

```
def join("game:" <> _player, _payload, socket) do
  {:ok, socket}
end
```

join/3 always takes a topic-subtopic string, some form of payload, and a socket struct. The return will either be {:ok, socket} or {:error, %{reason: "<whatever reason you like>"}}. This is slightly different from other return tuples we'll see in a minute, but the {:ok, socket} return is an echo of the {:ok, state} tuple we return from init/1 when starting a GenServer.

Now that we have a simple clause of the join/3 function, let's go to the IEx session we have running and compile our new GameChannel:

```
iex> c "lib/islands_interface_web/channels/game_channel.ex"
[IslandsInterfaceWeb.GameChannel]
```

Great—that's just what we wanted to see. Now we need to get a client to use join/3. For that, we'll need some JavaScript, and we'll write some in the next section.

Establish a Client Connection

Our goal in this section is to write client code that can invoke the join/3 function we now have on the server. There are a few steps we'll need to take to make that happen.

We'll need to define a client socket and use it to establish a connection to the socket on the server. Then we'll need to define a new channel object on the client, and use it to join the channel on the server.

Phoenix ships with phoenix.js, a JavaScript file that knows all about working with sockets and channels. It's indispensable for writing JavaScript client code for channels, and our first task is to make it available in the browser's console window.

Let's go to player1's JavaScript console—that's the browser window on the left—and require the phoenix.js file:

```
> var phoenix = require("phoenix")
undefined
```

Next we need to instantiate a new socket object so we can establish a connection from the client to the channel running on the server. As we do that, we need to pass it a path to the socket as well as any parameters we want to pass in as we establish a connection. We don't need to pass any in, so we use a blank object:

```
> var socket = new phoenix.Socket("/socket", {})
undefined
```

Once we have the socket object, we can have it establish a connection to the path we defined when we created it:

```
> socket.connect()
undefined
```

Now that we're connected, we need to define a new channel object before we're ready to start pushing messages down the server. To do that, we invoke the socket.channel function with the topic-subtopic, and some parameters.

The general form of that call looks like this:

```
> var new_channel = socket.channel("topic:subtopic", {some_key: "some_value"})
```

The parameters are important. The ones we specify here are the ones that will get passed to the join/3 function in the GameChannel, even if we pass other parameters into the client's join function later on.

```
def join("game:" <> _player, parameters, socket) do
```

To make this a little neater and more flexible, let's wrap that socket.channel call in a new function called new_channel. It will take a subtopic and the screen name of the player who wants to join. The one parameter we want to send into the channel object itself is the player's screen name.

Go ahead and type the function definitions in at player1's console prompt:

```
> function new_channel(subtopic, screen_name) {
  return socket.channel("game:" + subtopic, {screen_name: screen_name});
}
undefined
```

Now we can invoke the new_channel function with a player's name to generate a new channel object. This will already have the parameters we specified baked into it:

```
> var game_channel = new_channel("moon", "moon")
undefined
```

If we click on the game_channel object in the console to inspect it, we'll see the params object itself:

```
> game_channel
Channel
. . .
params: Object
  screen_name: "moon"
  __proto__: Object
. . .
```

That's exactly what we want.

There's one more function we'll need to define in player1's console, and that's the join function itself.

As a practical matter, the game_channel object already has a join function. We could call it directly, but the return value would be an object that, on the face of it, wouldn't tell us whether or not it worked.

In order to see that something is really happening in the JavaScript console, we'll define a wrapper function around the channel's join function:

```
> function join(channel) {
  channel.join()
    .receive("ok", response => {
      console.log("Joined successfully!", response)
    })
    .receive("error", response => {
      console.log("Unable to join", response)
    })
}
undefined
```

Inside our wrapper function, we chain receive function calls to check for a return of "ok" or "error" and log out a different message depending on which one we get.

Now that we have our own join function defined, we can invoke it, and if all goes well, that will invoke the join/3 function we wrote in the channel.

This message path is going to be from player1 to the channel and only back to player1, like this:

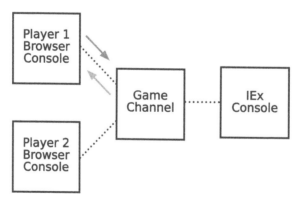

Let's try it out in player1's console:

```
> join(game_channel)
undefined
Joined successfully! Object {}
```

That worked!

Back in our IEx session, we'll see that the join call worked:

```
iex> JOIN game:moon to IslandsInterfaceWeb.GameChannel
  Transport:  Phoenix.Transports.WebSocket
  Parameters: %{"screen_name" => "moon"}
[info] Replied game:moon :ok
```

Clients can also leave a channel. We can give the same treatment to a leave function:

```
> function leave(channel) {
  channel.leave()
    .receive("ok", response => {
      console.log("Left successfully", response)
    })
    .receive("error", response => {
      console.log("Unable to leave", response)
    })
}
```

Now that we can get a client to join a channel on the server, we're ready to get a dialogue going between the client and the server.

Converse Over a Channel

This is where things start to get interesting. So far, we've sent a join message and gotten an ok back, but channels support much richer forms of bidirectional communications between clients and the server. We're going to take a closer look at the most common of these, and they will help us a lot through the rest of this chapter and while building your own applications.

The simplest way to send a message back from the server is to return a :reply tuple from the channel callback. This is a three-element tuple {:reply, some_response, socket}, where the middle element gets sent back to the client that originally sent the message. This should look really familiar after our work with GenServer.

Another way to talk back from a channel is with the push/3 function. push/3 sends the caller back a string that represents a new event along with a data payload. The caller needs to listen for that event, and we can define whatever actions to take in response to it that we want.

Broadcasting is another way for the server to send messages back to clients. The broadcast/3 and broadcast!/3 functions also send a string that represents a new event, along with a payload, but they send that event to every client that has subscribed to that specific topic-subtopic.

Let's take a look at reply tuples first. The path of the message passing will go from player1, to the channel on the server, and back to player1.

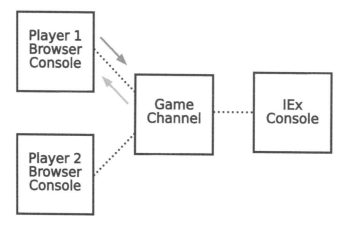

Just as we saw in OTP Behaviours, there's a mapping in channels between function calls and specific callbacks. When a channel object in the client calls the push function with a message and a payload, that triggers the handle_in/3 callback in the channel on the server.

Also as in OTP Behaviours, we'll define multiple clauses of handle_in/3 that each pattern match on a different message, or a different payload.

The first thing we'll need in the GameChannel is a clause of handle_in/3 that matches the message "hello" and replies with :ok:

```
def handle_in("hello", payload, socket) do
  {:reply, {:ok, payload}, socket}
end
```

Remember to recompile the GameChannel module in the IEx session—otherwise, this callback function won't exist in the running BEAM:

```
iex> r IslandsInterfaceWeb.GameChannel
warning: redefining module IslandsInterfaceWeb.GameChannel
(current version loaded from
_build/dev/lib/islands_interface/ebin/Elixir.IslandsInterfaceWeb.GameChannel.beam)
web/channels/game_channel.ex:1

{:reloaded, IslandsInterfaceWeb.GameChannel, [IslandsInterfaceWeb.GameChannel]}
```

We could trigger this callback from player1's console with game_channel.push(), but we would get an object back that wouldn't tell us much on first glance.

To see how this behaves more clearly, let's write another wrapper function in player1's console that will give us some feedback. For the payload, we'll pass a JavaScript object with a greeting:

```
> function say_hello(channel, greeting) {
  channel.push("hello", {"message": greeting})
    .receive("ok", response => {
       console.log("Hello", response.message)
     })
    .receive("error", response => {
       console.log("Unable to say hello to the channel.", response.message)
     })
}
undefined
```

Let's check out how this works in player1's console:

```
> say_hello(game_channel, "World!")
undefined
Hello World!
```

Of course, we can do anything we would like before we return the payload, as long as we adhere to the rules for the return value. We need to reply with either a status atom—:ok or :error—by itself, or a tagged tuple with a status atom and a map for the second element.

Just to prove that the error condition works, let's change the function to alter the payload and always return an error:

```
def handle_in("hello", payload, socket) do
  payload = %{message: "We forced this error."}
  {:reply, {:error, payload}, socket}
end
```

Go ahead and recompile the GameChannel in the IEx session.

Then let's go to player1's browser console and send a "hello" message to the channel again:

```
> say_hello(game_channel, "World!")
undefined
Unable to say hello to the channel. We forced this error.
```

Now let's take a look at how push/3 works inside the GameChannel. Instead of a reply tuple, this will send a new event down the channel, but only to the original caller. Since we're not relying on a reply tuple to communicate back to the client, we'll replace it with {:noreply, socket}.

The path of message passing will look the same as reply as shown in the figure on page 166.

Let's go to the channel and change the handle_in/3 clause to use push/3. We could leave the :reply tuple there and get two responses, but since push/3 will already send a reply, it makes more sense to swap in {:noreply, socket} instead.

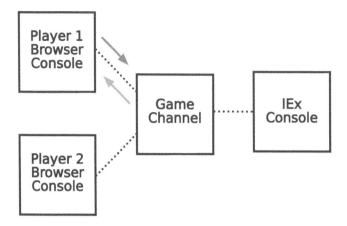

Let's recompile the GameChannel so we can see this in action:

```
def handle_in("hello", payload, socket) do
  push socket, "said_hello", payload
  {:noreply, socket}
end
```

Then let's head over to player1's console to give it a try:

```
> say_hello(game_channel, "World!")
undefined
```

And we get nothing.

Here's why. The handle_in/3 clause is pushing a new event, "said_hello", to the caller. The problem is that we don't have any code in the browser that is listening for that event.

We need to use the on function defined on the channel object to listen for the "said_hello" event and respond in a way we define. We'll just have it log "Returned Greeting" and send the response to the console.

Let's go ahead and define an event listener in player1's console and try again:

```
> game_channel.on("said_hello", response => {
    console.log("Returned Greeting:", response.message)
  })
undefined
```

```
> say_hello(game_channel, "World!")
undefined
Returned Greeting: World!
```

That's exactly what we want.

Now let's take a look at broadcast/3 or the bang version, broadcast!/3. The bang version will raise an exception if it fails. The non-bang version will return an error tuple instead.

The message path for broadcast is going to look a little different. The message will originate from player1 to the channel, but the channel will send event messages to both player1 and player2.

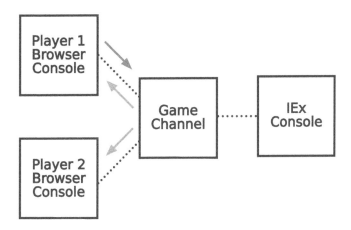

This will also send an event, which is the second argument after the socket, to all members who have joined the channel.

Let's use the bang version to simplify our code. We can change our "hello" clause of handle_in/3 to look like this:

```
def handle_in("hello", payload, socket) do
  broadcast! socket, "said_hello", payload
  {:noreply, socket}
end
```

Since we're going to broadcast an event to all users who have joined the channel instead of returning a reply, use the {:noreply, socket} return value.

Now to see this really work, let's go over to player2's console and get it set up to communicate over the channel. We'll need to do all the setup we did before—requiring the Phoenix.js file, defining a socket, connecting, and joining the channel.

```
> var phoenix = require("phoenix")
undefined

> var socket = new phoenix.Socket("/socket", {})
undefined
```

```
> socket.connect()
undefined

> function new_channel(player, screen_name) {
 return socket.channel("game:" + player, {screen_name: screen_name});
}
undefined

function join(channel) {
  channel.join()
    .receive("ok", response => {
       console.log("Joined successfully!", response)
     })
    .receive("error", response => {
       console.log("Unable to join", response)
     })
}
undefined
```

We want to be sure to communicate on exactly the same topic-subtopic, so we pass in the same name, "moon", to the join function that we did in player1's console. But this is a different player, so we pass in a different screen name.

```
> var game_channel = new_channel("moon", "diva")
undefined

> join(game_channel)
undefined
Joined successfully Object {}
```

Now we need to make sure that player2's console is listening for the "said_hello" event, just like player1:

```
> game_channel.on("said_hello", response => {
    console.log("Returned Greeting", response.message)
  })
undefined
```

Now for the interesting part. Let's go back to player1's console and say hello again:

```
> say_hello(game_channel, "World!")
undefined
Returned Greeting: World!
```

Great—it caught the event. If we take a look at player2's console, we'll see that it caught the same event.

That's exactly what we want to see.

Connect the Channel to the Game

Here's where we begin to do the real work of getting our new game channel talking to the game server. We're going to build out new clauses of handle_in/3 that correspond to the public interface functions we wrote for IslandsEngine.Game. We'll pick the right communication strategy for each action, and we'll continue to check our work at each step, both in the browser consoles and in IEx.

The mechanics of making these connections is so easy, it's going to feel like cheating. When we're done, all the actions a player can take in the game will be exposed on the web through a channel interface.

For all of these new actions, we're going to follow the same pattern we used for the "hello" function. We'll define a new clause of handle_in/3 that calls directly to the game server, define a function in the browser console that pushes a message to that clause, call the function, and check the response.

Now that we're talking to the game server, though, we have the opportunity to check the game server state before and after we call the function in the console to make sure that the action worked.

We're ready to go, and the place to begin is with initializing a new game.

Start a New Game

This is where we begin to expose the actual game to the web. We'll start with a clause of handle_in/3 that will match on the "new_game" action. Within that function, we'll call directly into the GameSupervisor.start_game/1 function to start the game, and report back on the success or failure to start the GenServer.

All we need to start a new game is the first player's name. We decided in this chapter that the first player's name will also be the subtopic of the channel. Because of that, we don't need to pass in the player's name to start the game—we can derive it from the topic stored on the socket struct.

Since there will be only one player at this point, we need to respond only to that one player. Sending back a :reply tuple fits the bill.

```
def handle_in("new_game", _payload, socket) do
  "game:" <> player = socket.topic
  case GameSupervisor.start_game(player) do
    {:ok, _pid} ->
      {:reply, :ok, socket}
    {:error, reason} ->
      {:reply, {:error, %{reason: reason}}, socket}
  end
end
```

Before we try this in the browser, let's make sure that the game server process hasn't yet been started.

Head over to the IEx session we have running and check for a game process named after the first player who joined the channel. We'll also need to recompile the GameChannel.

```
iex> alias IslandsEngine.Game
IslandsEngine.Game

iex> via = Game.via_tuple("moon")
{:via, Registry, {Registry.Game, "moon"}}

iex> GenServer.whereis(via)
nil
```

Fantastic. There is no process with that global name.

Back in player1's browser console, let's define a new function that will push the "new_game" message to the channel:

```
> function new_game(channel) {
 channel.push("new_game")
   .receive("ok", response => {
      console.log("New Game!", response)
    })
   .receive("error", response => {
      console.log("Unable to start a new game.", response)
    })
}
undefined
```

And when we call that function in player1's console, it works!

```
> new_game(game_channel)
undefined
New Game! Object {}
```

Now let's check back in IEx to see if the game process exists:

```
iex> GenServer.whereis(via)
#PID<0.402.0>
```

Great! We started a new game from the browser.

Now let's see what happens when we do something we know will fail, like starting a game with the same name. Recall that we can start only one game with the same name at a time.

```
> new_game(game_channel)
undefined
Joined successfully Object {}
```

That's strange. The console says that we rejoined.

This happens because the channel crashed. After the crash, the client tried, and succeeded, to reconnect.

But why did the channel crash? Won't GenServer throw a polite error if we try to start another game with the same name? Yes, it will, but the polite error it throws includes a PID. Poison, the JSON encoder, doesn't know how to encode PIDs. Let's take a look back at the IEx console to see the evidence:

```
[error] GenServer #PID<0.375.0> terminating
** (Poison.EncodeError) unable to encode value:
            {:already_started, #PID<0.376.0>}
    . . .
```

The easiest thing we can do to fix this is just pass the reason for the error through the inspect/1 function in the error reply. Then the handle_in/3 for new_game would look like this:

channel/lib/islands_interface_web/game_channel.ex
```
def handle_in("new_game", _payload, socket) do
  "game:" <> player = socket.topic
  case GameSupervisor.start_game(player) do
    {:ok, _pid} ->
      {:reply, :ok, socket}
    {:error, reason} ->
      {:reply, {:error, %{reason: inspect(reason)}}, socket}
  end
end
```

After we recompile the game channel and try to start the game twice, we get an entirely different result:

```
> new_game(game)
undefined
Unable to start a new game.
Object {reason: "{:already_started, #PID<0.386.0>}"}
```

That's much nicer.

Now it's time to work on adding a second player.

Add a Second Player

In order to add a second player, we just need to pass that player's name to the Game.add_player/2 function along with the via tuple that maps to the game PID.

Successfully adding a second player is something we want both players to know about. But if we fail to add the second player, only that player really needs to know. This is a case where we can use broadcast!/3 on success, and :reply tuple if something goes wrong.

Fortunately, we have an easy way of deriving the via tuple to address the right game process. The socket.topic will always be a string that begins with "game:" and ends with the first player's name. We can do a little binary pattern matching to extract just the name. That player's name is all we need to get the via tuple from Game.via_tuple/1.

channel/lib/islands_interface_web/game_channel.ex
```
defp via("game:" <> player), do: Game.via_tuple(player)
```

With that information, let's define a new handle_in/3 clause for the "add_player" action:

channel/lib/islands_interface_web/game_channel.ex
```
def handle_in("add_player", player, socket) do
  case Game.add_player(via(socket.topic), player) do
    :ok ->
      broadcast! socket, "player_added", %{message:
      "New player just joined: " <> player}
      {:noreply, socket}
    {:error, reason} ->
      {:reply, {:error, %{reason: inspect(reason)}}, socket}
    :error -> {:reply, :error, socket}
  end
end
```

Now let's go over to player2's browser console and add a function to push the "add_player" message to the channel, with the new player's name as the payload:

```
> function add_player(channel, player) {
  channel.push("add_player", player)
    .receive("error", response => {
      console.log("Unable to add new player: " + player, response)
    })
}
undefined
```

In order to catch the "player_added" event on the channel, in the case where we are successful, we need to add a new on function to the game channel.

Let's add this to both players' browser consoles:

```
> game_channel.on("player_added", response => {
    console.log("Player Added", response)
  })
undefined
```

Now we can go back to the IEx session to check the state of the game. Since we've got a new game started, player1 should already have the name "moon", but player2 should not yet have a name.

```
iex> state_data = :sys.get_state(via)
. . .

iex> state_data.player1.name
"moon"

iex> state_data.player2.name
nil
```

That's exactly what we wanted. In the second player's browser console, let's actually add the second player:

```
> add_player(game_channel, "diva")
undefined
Player Added Object {message: "New player just joined: diva"}
```

Nice! We've captured the "player_added" event and logged its message to the console. If we check in the first player's browser console, we should see the message there as well.

Finally, let's take a look at the game state in IEx to make sure that player2 has a name:

```
iex> state_data = :sys.get_state(via)
. . .

iex> state_data.player1.name
"moon"

iex> state_data.player2.name
"diva"
```

Yes, that worked exactly the way we expected it to. Now let's move on to setting an island's coordinates.

Positioning Islands

Positioning islands requires a player, an island key, and the row and column values of the upper-left coordinate. This is an action that needs to be secret, for the eyes of the player setting her island coordinate only. Giving that information away is like giving the game away.

As we define a new handle_in/3 clause to do this, we're going to use a :reply tuple, so that only the player setting his island's coordinates will see the response.

The "position_island" message originates in JavaScript. JavaScript doesn't have an atom type, so we'll send the player and island key values over as strings.

That means we'll need to convert them to atoms in the handle_in/3 function before we pass them into the game server.

Atoms are really appropriate in the Elixir world, but they don't exist in Java-Script. We're okay doing these translations here because this is a boundary of the system. There won't be any other way to interact with the game engine from the web.

channel/lib/islands_interface_web/game_channel.ex
```elixir
def handle_in("position_island", payload, socket) do
  %{"player" => player, "island" => island,
    "row" => row, "col" => col} = payload
  player = String.to_existing_atom(player)
  island = String.to_existing_atom(island)
  case Game.position_island(via(socket.topic), player, island, row, col) do
    :ok -> {:reply, :ok, socket}
    _ -> {:reply, :error, socket}
  end
end
```

Atoms and User-Generated Content

Using String.to_existing_atom/1 to convert user-generated strings into atoms closes an attack vector. This function will do the conversion only if the atom already exists in the system, and it will throw an error if the atom doesn't currently exist.

The BEAM has a hard limit on the number of atoms it allows, and it never garbage-collects them. If we didn't convert to only preexisting atoms, malicious players could write a script to flood the system with previously nonexistent players and island types, which would crash the BEAM.

As we have with all these new actions so far, we'll need a new function to wrap the channel.push call and show us what the result is. Let's add this to both players' browser consoles:

```javascript
> function position_island(channel, player, island, row, col) {
  var params = {"player": player, "island": island, "row": row, "col": col}
  channel.push("position_island", params)
    .receive("ok", response => {
      console.log("Island positioned!", response)
    })
    .receive("error", response => {
      console.log("Unable to position island.", response)
    })
}
undefined
```

Before we set coordinates in any islands, let's take a look at player2's board:

```
iex> state_data = :sys.get_state(via)
. . .

iex> state_data.player2.board
%{}
```

Excellent! All of player2's islands are empty, as we would expect.

Let's go to player2's console and position an "atoll" island at row 1, column 1:

```
> position_island(game_channel, "player2", "atoll", 1, 1)
undefined
Island positioned! Object {}
```

Success! Now let's go to the IEx console and see if it really worked:

```
iex> state_data = :sys.get_state(via)
. . .

iex> state_data.player2.board
%{atoll:
  %IslandsEngine.Island{
    coordinates: #MapSet<[
      %IslandsEngine.Coordinate{col: 1, row: 1},
      %IslandsEngine.Coordinate{col: 1, row: 3},
      %IslandsEngine.Coordinate{col: 2, row: 1},
      %IslandsEngine.Coordinate{col: 2, row: 2},
      %IslandsEngine.Coordinate{col: 2, row: 3}
    ]>,
    hit_coordinates: #MapSet<[]>
  }
}
```

It did work. Player2's board clearly has an atoll positioned.

Before we move on to setting islands, let's get the game state ready for it. The rules check to make sure that a player has all of his islands positioned before it will allow that player to set his islands. Player2 already has an atoll positioned, so let's go ahead and position all of player2's other islands:

```
> position_island(game_channel, "player2", "dot", 1, 5)
undefined
Island positioned! Object {}

> position_island(game_channel, "player2", "l_shape", 1, 7)
undefined
Island positioned! Object {}

> position_island(game_channel, "player2", "s_shape", 5, 1)
undefined
Island positioned! Object {}
```

```
> position_island(game_channel, "player2", "square", 5, 5)
undefined
Island positioned! Object {}
```

Then let's populate one of player1's islands from her console:

```
> position_island(game_channel, "player1", "dot", 1, 1)
undefined
Island positioned! Object {}
```

With that, we're ready to move on to setting players' islands.

Setting Islands

Once players are done moving their islands around, they need to mark their islands as set in place. All the channel needs to do is pass an atom representing the player down to Game.set_islands/2 and pattern match on the result to send the right response.

A player successfully setting his islands is something we want both players to know about, so we will use broadcast!/3 to respond when Game.set_islands/2 succeeds. If it fails, we want to let only that player know, so we use a :reply tuple.

In order to make it easier for any front-end code to display all the islands once they are successfully set, we will also have to send a :reply tuple with the full map of islands, but just to the caller. We would not want the opponent to see this!

channel/lib/islands_interface_web/game_channel.ex
```
def handle_in("set_islands", player, socket) do
  player = String.to_existing_atom(player)
  case Game.set_islands(via(socket.topic), player) do
    {:ok, board} ->
      broadcast! socket, "player_set_islands", %{player: player}
      {:reply, {:ok, %{board: board}}, socket}
    _ -> {:reply, :error, socket}
  end
end
```

We'll need to transform the player from a string into an atom again because that's what the game server expects.

Now let's add a function wrapping the channel.push call to the server. If the function succeeds, the player that sent the message will receive an "ok" response, which will include the board as its payload. Let's log both of those to the console. Let's go ahead and add this to both players' consoles:

```
> function set_islands(channel, player) {
 channel.push("set_islands", player)
   .receive("ok", response => {
     console.log("Here is the board:");
     console.dir(response.board);
   })
   .receive("error", response => {
       console.log("Unable to set islands for: " + player, response)
     })
}
undefined
```

We'll also need to listen for the "player_set_islands" event the server will broadcast on success. We'll need this in both players' consoles as well:

```
> game_channel.on("player_set_islands", response => {
    console.log("Player Set Islands", response)
  })
undefined
```

There won't be any changes in the game server state to check here, but the rules struct will change along the way. Let's check in with that in the IEx session. We would expect the state machine to be in the :players_set state at this point, and we would expect it to stay there until both players have set their islands.

```
iex> state_data = :sys.get_state(via)

. . .

iex> state_data.rules.state
:players_set
```

That's exactly what we expected.

Now let's call the set_islands function in player2's browser window:

```
> set_islands(game_channel, "player2")
undefined
Player Set Islands Object {player: "player2"}

Here is the board:
Object
  > atoll: Object
  > dot: Object
  > l_shape: Object
  > s_shape: Object
  > square: Object
  > __proto__: Object
```

Great. We got the "player_set_islands" event signifying success. We should also see the same response in player1's console.

Now let's check back with the state machine in the the IEx session. It should still be in the :players_set state.

```
iex> state_data = :sys.get_state(via)
. . .

iex> state_data.rules.state
:players_set
```

Nice—that's just what we expected to see.

Now that we can set a player's islands, we're off to guessing coordinates, the last and arguably most important part of playing the game.

Before we move on, we're going to cheat a little. Normally both players would need to position all their islands and then set them before either player could guess. Showing a win would require *a lot* of guesses.

Currently, player2 has positioned and set his islands, but player1 has positioned only her dot island. If we manually reset the state to :player1_turn, player1 can begin guessing, and player2 can win with a single correct guess.

We're going to reference the rules struct, so let's alias the Rules module first:

```
iex> alias IslandsEngine.Rules
IslandsEngine.Rules

iex> state_data = :sys.get_state(via)
. . .

iex> state_data = :sys.replace_state(via, fn state_data ->
...>   %{state_data | rules: %Rules{state: :player1_turn}}
...> end)
. . .

iex> state_data.rules.state
:player1_turn
```

With that out of the way, we're ready to tackle guessing coordinates.

Guessing Coordinates

For this final piece, we'll need to pass a player and a coordinate into Game.guess_coordinate/3. We should show the result of a successful guess to both players, so we'll broadcast those. If a guess fails, we'll return a :reply tuple.

That's exactly what we've done for the past few handle_in/3 clauses, but this one has a twist. The response we'll get back from Game.guess_coordinate/3 will be a tuple, but we need to use a map for the payload of our broadcast. That means that we'll need to do a little pattern matching to destructure the tuple and build it back up again as a map.

channel/lib/islands_interface_web/game_channel.ex
```elixir
def handle_in("guess_coordinate", params, socket) do
  %{"player" => player, "row" => row, "col" => col} = params
  player = String.to_existing_atom(player)
  case Game.guess_coordinate(via(socket.topic), player, row, col) do
    {:hit, island, win} ->
      result = %{hit: true, island: island, win: win}
      broadcast! socket, "player_guessed_coordinate",
                 %{player: player, row: row, col: col, result: result}
      {:noreply, socket}
    {:miss, island, win} ->
      result = %{hit: false, island: island, win: win}
      broadcast! socket, "player_guessed_coordinate",
                 %{player: player, row: row, col: col, result: result}
      {:noreply, socket}
    :error ->
      {:reply, {:error, %{player: player, reason: "Not your turn."}}, socket}
    {:error, reason} ->
      {:reply, {:error, %{player: player, reason: reason}}, socket}
  end
end
```

Great! Now let's add a wrapper function to push this message to the channel. We'll need it in both players' consoles.

```javascript
> function guess_coordinate(channel, player, row, col) {
  var params = {"player": player, "row": row, "col": col}
  channel.push("guess_coordinate", params)
    .receive("error", response => {
        console.log("Unable to guess a coordinate: " + player, response)
    })
}
undefined
```

Since we're broadcasting from the handle_in/3 on success, we need to listen for the "player_guessed_coordinate" event in both players' consoles:

```javascript
> game_channel.on("player_guessed_coordinate", response => {
    console.log("Player Guessed Coordinate: ", response.result)
  })
undefined
```

We've manually set the state to be :player1_turn, so let's have player1 make an incorrect guess to start with. We just positioned all of player2's islands, and the highest row we put them in was 5, so any guess in row 10 will miss.

```javascript
> guess_coordinate(game_channel, "player1", 10, 1)
undefined
Player Guessed Coordinate:  player1
      Object {win: "no_win", island: "none", hit: false}
```

That tells us all the right things. It wasn't a hit, no island was forested, and it didn't result in a win.

Let's check player1's guesses in IEx one more time to make sure they still look right:

```
iex> state_data = :sys.get_state(via)
. . .
```

```
iex> state_data.player1.guesses
%IslandsEngine.Guesses{hits: #MapSet<[]>,
 misses: #MapSet<[%IslandsEngine.Coordinate{col: 1, row: 10}]>}
```

That's correct. Now it's player2's turn to guess. Player1 positioned a single dot island at row 1, column 1. If we have player2 guess it, then player2 should win.

```
> guess_coordinate(game_channel, "player2", 1, 1)
undefined
Player Guessed Coordinate:  player2
       Object {win: "win", island: "dot", hit: true}
```

Player2 does in fact win. That should have transitioned the game state to :game_over. Let's check to make sure:

```
iex> state_data = :sys.get_state(via)
. . .
```

```
iex> state_data.rules.state
:game_over
```

That's exactly what we should have seen. That wraps up all the functionality the game itself needs. We could call the channel done if we wanted to and people could still play the game.

There's one nagging little bit, though. We said early on that each game should be private to two players. We currently don't have a way to limit the number of players who can join the channel on a given topic-subtopic combination.

Phoenix Presence is going to help us out with this, and that's where we're going next.

Phoenix Presence

From the earliest days of Phoenix channels, developers have asked how to tell who is currently subscribed to a channel. Until recently, the answer was to create a custom solution that best fits an individual application's circumstances. But now, we have Phoenix Presence to solve that problem in a general way for all of us.

Presence has one job to do: to keep track of the clients subscribed to a topic on a channel. For us, that means keeping track of the players in each game. Presence does this amazingly well. This might sound like a trivial task, but it's deceptively difficult.

If you were to roll your own version of Presence, your first thought might be to maintain a list of the subscribers, adding clients to the list when they join and removing them when they leave. This might work for a system with a single node.

With a single data structure on multiple nodes, though, you would have to make sure that the data is available to all nodes in the cluster. But nodes don't stay up forever, and a crash could lose all of the subscription data.

You could put the data in an external database to solve that data durability problem, but then network hiccups could disrupt communication to the database, and the system would miss clients joining or leaving. That would make the data out of sync with the real state of the channel.

The scenarios only get more complex from there. Add in users subscribing to the same topic from multiple devices as well as flakey mobile connections, and a solid solution might seem evasive indeed.

That's where CRDTs (conflict-free replicated datatypes) come to the rescue. They track the sequence of clients joining and leaving, across nodes and clients. They do it without relying on clock time, which can drift from machine to machine. CRDTs allow Presence to reconstruct the sequence of events to accurately determine which clients are currently subscribed to a topic on a channel.

In the future, this job might even be expanded to keep track of other things that can join or leave a group, like nodes, services, and processes. Stay tuned!

The power of Phoenix Presence is compounded by how easy it is to set up and use. We'll need a new and mostly empty Presence module, and we'll need to make sure that it's started when IslandsInterface is.

After that, we'll need a single callback function in the channel to make it work, though we'll add another just to help us see Presence in action.

The plan is that as a player is joining, before we return {:ok, socket}, the channel will send itself a message with the player's screen name. The first callback we write will match that message and have Presence start tracking that screen name.

The browser consoles we've been using are already full of state from playing a game. Let's start with a clean slate by shutting the server down and reloading both players' windows.

We need to begin with an empty Presence module in our application. Let's put it in lib/islands_interface_web/channels/presence.ex:

```
defmodule IslandsInterfaceWeb.Presence do
  use Phoenix.Presence, otp_app: :islands_interface,
                        pubsub_server: IslandsInterface.PubSub
end
```

This module brings in Phoenix.Presence, specifies our Application name, and specifies which PubSub server we'll use. We're using the one that Phoenix provided for us when we generated the project.

We won't need to add anything to this module. It's fine as it is.

Next we need to make sure that the Presence module gets started in our supervision tree when we start the application. Open up lib/islands_interface/application.ex and add the Presence module in the list of children:

```
children = [
  supervisor(IslandsInterfaceWeb.Endpoint, []),
  supervisor(IslandsInterfaceWeb.Presence, []),
]
```

That's it for the application setup. Hardly anything to it.

Before we can begin to use Presence, in the GameChannel, we'll need to alias it:

```
alias IslandsInterfaceWeb.Presence
```

Now we need a single callback in game_channel.ex. In order to handle a raw message the channel will send to itself, we'll use a handle_info/2 callback. We'll have this callback match on {:after_join, player_name}.

```
channel/lib/islands_interface_web/game_channel.ex
def handle_info({:after_join, screen_name}, socket) do
  {:ok, _} = Presence.track(socket, screen_name, %{
    online_at: inspect(System.system_time(:seconds))
  })
  {:noreply, socket}
end
```

The body of the callback tells Presence to start tracking this user by her screen name, and notes when that user joined the channel.

The way we trigger that callback is by having the channel send itself the {:after_join, screen_name} message we matched for in the handle_info/2 callback.

```
def join("game:" <> _player, %{"screen_name" => screen_name}, socket) do
  send(self(), {:after_join, screen_name})
  {:ok, socket}
end
```

In order to see Presence info from the browser, though, we'll need another handle_in clause that will broadcast the list of players that Presence is currently tracking:

channel/lib/islands_interface_web/game_channel.ex
```
def handle_in("show_subscribers", _payload, socket) do
  broadcast! socket, "subscribers", Presence.list(socket)
  {:noreply, socket}
end
```

Then we'll need to listen for and respond to the "subscribers" event in both players' consoles. Go ahead and recompile the IslandsInterfaceWeb.GameChannel module in the IEx console. Then let's test this out. In each player's browser console, let's begin to set up the state, just as we did before:

```
> var phoenix = require("phoenix")
undefined

> var socket = new phoenix.Socket("/socket", {})
undefined

> socket.connect()
undefined

> function new_channel(player, screen_name) {
 return socket.channel("game:" + player, {screen_name: screen_name});
}
undefined

> function join(channel) {
  channel.join()
    .receive("ok", response => {
      console.log("Joined successfully!", response)
    })
    .receive("error", response => { console.log("Unable to join", response) })
}
undefined
```

Then in player1's console, let's create a new channel object and listen for the "subscribers" event:

```
> var game_channel = new_channel("moon", "moon")
undefined

> game_channel.on("subscribers", response => {
    console.log("These players have joined: ", response)
  })
undefined
```

Now let's do the same thing for player2 in his console, but this time changing the arguments to new_channel:

```
> var game_channel = new_channel("moon", "diva")
undefined

> game_channel.on("subscribers", response => {
    console.log("These players have joined: ", response)
  })
undefined
```

With both players set up, let's have player1 join the channel. After player1 joins, we can push the "show_subscribers" message over the channel:

```
> join(game_channel)
undefined
Joined successfully! Object {}

> game_channel.push("show_subscribers")
. . .
These players have joined:  Object {moon: Object}
```

That correctly tells us that the first player has joined. Nice.

Even though we are broadcasting from the channel, we will not yet see the logged message in player2's console because that player has not joined the channel yet.

Let's take care of that now:

```
> join(game_channel)
undefined
Joined successfully! Object {}

> game_channel.push("show_subscribers")
. . .
These players have joined:  Object {moon: Object, diva: Object}
```

That's perfect. In player2's console, we see a message telling us that both players have joined. Since player1 had joined previously, that player will see this logged message as well.

Now that we can tell which players are subscribed to a channel on a given topic, we can implement the one last feature we need: authorization.

Authorization

In this last section, we'll be tackling authorization—deciding if an action is permissible. The action we really care about is joining a channel. The rules for this are simple. We want only two players to join a channel on any given topic-subtopic, and we want those two players to have different screen names.

Authentication Resources

In Islands, we don't have any need for authentication—determining if users are who they say they are. If your application does need authentication, there are resources out there to help. Check out the documentation for Phoenix.Token if you need token-based authentication. Alternately, *Programming Phoenix* by Chris McCord, José Valim, and Bruce Tate has a lot of great information on authentication.

Now that we have Presence, we can write functions to check both of the authorization conditions we outlined, and we can roll them up into a single function that determines whether a given player can join.

The first condition we need to check is how many players have already joined the channel. Presence.list/1 returns a map. The keys of this map are the screen names of all the players who have joined the channel on a specific topic-subtopic. We can write a function to return that number by getting the Presence list and counting the keys.

channel/lib/islands_interface_web/game_channel.ex
```elixir
defp number_of_players(socket) do
  socket
  |> Presence.list()
  |> Map.keys()
  |> length()
end
```

We can also tell if a player is already subscribed to this game channel by seeing if a given screen name is already a key in the Presence map.

channel/lib/islands_interface_web/game_channel.ex
```elixir
defp existing_player?(socket, screen_name) do
  socket
  |> Presence.list()
  |> Map.has_key?(screen_name)
end
```

With those two functions, we have enough information to see if a player is authorized to join the channel:

channel/lib/islands_interface_web/game_channel.ex
```elixir
defp authorized?(socket, screen_name) do
  number_of_players(socket) < 2 && !existing_player?(socket, screen_name)
end
```

Now we can use this authorized?/2 function in join/3 to decide if we should let a new player join.

channel/lib/islands_interface_web/game_channel.ex
```
def join("game:" <> _player, %{"screen_name" => screen_name}, socket) do
  if authorized?(socket, screen_name)  do
    send(self(), {:after_join, screen_name})
    {:ok, socket}
  else
    {:error, %{reason: "unauthorized"}}
  end
end
```

To see this in action, let's stop the server and reload the two browser windows again, just to start from a clean slate. Then let's open a third window representing a third player who will not be able to join.

In each of the three browser consoles, go ahead and set up the state and functions that we'll need:

```
> var phoenix = require("phoenix")
undefined

> var socket = new phoenix.Socket("/socket", {})
undefined

> socket.connect()
undefined

> function new_channel(player, screen_name) {
 return socket.channel("game:" + player, {screen_name: screen_name});
}
undefined

> function join(channel) {
  channel.join()
    .receive("ok", response => {
      console.log("Joined successfully!", response)
    })
    .receive("error", response => { console.log("Unable to join", response) })
}
undefined
```

Now let's have each player instantiate a new channel object and try to join the channel, starting with player1. What we're expecting is that player1 and player2 will be able to join, but the third player won't:

```
> var game_channel = new_channel("moon", "moon")
undefined

> join(game_channel)
undefined
Joined successfully! Object {}
```

Player1 joined successfully.

Now let's try player2.

```
> var game_channel = new_channel("moon", "diva")
undefined

> join(game_channel)
undefined
Joined successfully! Object {}
```

Player2 joined without a problem, so let's try the third player in the new browser console.

```
> var game_channel = new_channel("moon", "nope")
undefined

> join(game_channel)
undefined
Unable to join Object {reason: "unauthorized"}
```

Great! As we expected, the third player wasn't allowed to join.

That's all the behavior we'll need from our channel.

This brings us right up to the boundary of conventional front-end web development. The steps that remain are to model the game state, render the player and opponent boards for each player, and map DOM events to the functions we just wrote, updating the game state appropriately along the way.

There's nothing revolutionary from here on out, and there are a number of sources available that show you how to do it in the front-end language and framework of your choice.

We won't leave you hanging, though. We've included the code for a demo front-end application written in React.js in the code bundle for the book. You can add that code to the islands_interface project and play through a game on your local machine.

Wrapping Up

Congratulations! You've made it.

You've built a Phoenix channel that provides an interface to the game engine you wrote in Part 1. You did it without coupling the logic to the interface in any way. The game engine concerns itself entirely with the business logic of the game. The channel concerns itself entirely with brokering messages between clients and the game engine.

You've seen how to use Phoenix Presence to track clients who have subscribed to a channel on a topic, and you've seen how to use that to implement an authorization scheme for joining the channel.

With that, we've completed the last layer we're going to cover in this book. Now go build some amazing new web apps!

Installing System Dependencies

Working through the examples in the book yourself is the best way to absorb the ideas. Having the right versions of the right software installed on your system will ease your way. You'll need Elixir first and foremost, and Elixir depends on Erlang. You'll also need the Phoenix installer to generate a new Phoenix interface, and you'll need Node.js and NPM to manage your front-end dependencies and assets.

Elixir

The Elixir site has great instructions on installing the latest Elixir for practically any system.[1] All the code in this book has been written with Elixir 1.5.1. For the best results, install a version equal to or greater than that.

If the installer prompts you to install Hex or Rebar 3, go ahead and say yes.

You can verify that the installation was successful by checking the Elixir version number:

```
$ elixir -v
Erlang/OTP 20 [erts-9.0] [source] [64-bit] [smp:8:8] [ds:8:8:10]
            [async-threads:10] [hipe] [kernel-poll:false] [dtrace]

Elixir 1.5.1
```

Erlang

Elixir depends on Erlang, so you'll need that too. In many cases, installing Elixir through a package management system will install Erlang as well. If you've installed Elixir but don't yet have Erlang, head to the downloads section

---

1. http://elixir-lang.org

of the Erlang website to find installation instructions for your system.[2] You'll want version 20 or greater to work with Elixir 1.5.

You can check the Erlang installation by opening up erl, the Erlang shell:

```
$ erl
Erlang/OTP 20 [erts-9.0] [source] [64-bit] [smp:8:8] [ds:8:8:10]
            [async-threads:10] [hipe] [kernel-poll:false] [dtrace]

Eshell V9.0  (abort with ^G)
```

Phoenix

You'll need the Phoenix installer archive as well. This is essentially the Mix command that allows us to generate a new Phoenix project. There's a single, albeit long, command to do this:

mix archive.install https://github.com/phoenixframework/archives/raw/master/phx_new.ez

That command just installed a Mix archive locally. Mix archives package up Elixir projects and allow us to run their Mix tasks. The particular task we're looking for is phx.new, which generates a new Phoenix project in much the same way that mix new generates a vanilla Elixir project.

Node.js and NPM

Phoenix uses Brunch to compile front-end assets like JavaScript and CSS files. Brunch requires NPM, the Node.js package manager bundled with Node.js. The easiest way to fulfill this dependency is to install Node.js version 5.0 or greater. Installation instructions are available at the Node.js site.[3]

With all of our installation complete, we're ready to get to work.

---

2. http://www.erlang.org
3. https://nodejs.org

Bibliography

[Tho16]   Dave Thomas. *Programming Elixir 1.3*. The Pragmatic Bookshelf, Raleigh, NC, 2016.

[TV16]   Chris McCord, Bruce Tate, and José Valim. *Programming Phoenix*. The Pragmatic Bookshelf, Raleigh, NC, 2016.

Index

Thank you!

How did you enjoy this book? Please let us know. Take a moment and email us at support@pragprog.com with your feedback. Tell us your story and you could win free ebooks. Please use the subject line "Book Feedback."

Ready for your next great Pragmatic Bookshelf book? Come on over to https://pragprog.com and use the coupon code BUYANOTHER2017 to save 30% on your next ebook.

Void where prohibited, restricted, or otherwise unwelcome. Do not use ebooks near water. If rash persists, see a doctor. Doesn't apply to *The Pragmatic Programmer* ebook because it's older than the Pragmatic Bookshelf itself. Side effects may include increased knowledge and skill, increased marketability, and deep satisfaction. Increase dosage regularly.

And thank you for your continued support,

Andy Hunt, Publisher

SAVE 30%!
Use coupon code
BUYANOTHER2017

Put the "Fun" in Functional

Elixir puts the "fun" back into functional programming, on top of the robust, battle-tested, industrial-strength environment of Erlang. Add in the unparalleled beauty and ease of the Phoenix web framework, and enjoy the web again!

Programming Elixir ≥ 1.6

This book is *the* introduction to Elixir for experienced programmers, completely updated for Elixir 1.6 and beyond. Explore functional programming without the academic overtones (tell me about monads just one more time). Create concurrent applications, but get them right without all the locking and consistency headaches. Meet Elixir, a modern, functional, concurrent language built on the rock-solid Erlang VM. Elixir's pragmatic syntax and built-in support for metaprogramming will make you productive and keep you interested for the long haul. Maybe the time is right for the Next Big Thing. Maybe it's Elixir.

Dave Thomas
(398 pages) ISBN: 9781680502992. $47.95
https://pragprog.com/book/elixir16

Programming Phoenix

Don't accept the compromise between fast and beautiful: you can have it all. Phoenix creator Chris McCord, Elixir creator José Valim, and award-winning author Bruce Tate walk you through building an application that's fast and reliable. At every step, you'll learn from the Phoenix creators not just what to do, but why. Packed with insider insights, this definitive guide will be your constant companion in your journey from Phoenix novice to expert, as you build the next generation of web applications.

Chris McCord, Bruce Tate, and José Valim
(298 pages) ISBN: 9781680501452. $34
https://pragprog.com/book/phoenix

Long Live the Command Line!

Use tmux and Vim for incredible mouse-free productivity.

tmux 2

Your mouse is slowing you down. The time you spend context switching between your editor and your consoles eats away at your productivity. Take control of your environment with tmux, a terminal multiplexer that you can tailor to your workflow. With this updated second edition for tmux 2.3, you'll customize, script, and leverage tmux's unique abilities to craft a productive terminal environment that lets you keep your fingers on your keyboard's home row.

Brian P. Hogan
(102 pages) ISBN: 9781680502213. $21.95
https://pragprog.com/book/bhtmux2

Modern Vim

Turn Vim into a full-blown development environment using Vim 8's new features and this sequel to the beloved bestseller *Practical Vim*. Integrate your editor with tools for building, testing, linting, indexing, and searching your codebase. Discover the future of Vim with Neovim: a fork of Vim that includes a built-in terminal emulator that will transform your workflow. Whether you choose to switch to Neovim or stick with Vim 8, you'll be a better developer.

Drew Neil
(190 pages) ISBN: 9781680502626. $39.95
https://pragprog.com/book/modvim

The Pragmatic Bookshelf

The Pragmatic Bookshelf features books written by developers for developers. The titles continue the well-known Pragmatic Programmer style and continue to garner awards and rave reviews. As development gets more and more difficult, the Pragmatic Programmers will be there with more titles and products to help you stay on top of your game.

Visit Us Online

This Book's Home Page
https://pragprog.com/book/lhelph
Source code from this book, errata, and other resources. Come give us feedback, too!

Register for Updates
https://pragprog.com/updates
Be notified when updates and new books become available.

Join the Community
https://pragprog.com/community
Read our weblogs, join our online discussions, participate in our mailing list, interact with our wiki, and benefit from the experience of other Pragmatic Programmers.

New and Noteworthy
https://pragprog.com/news
Check out the latest pragmatic developments, new titles and other offerings.

Save on the eBook

Save on the eBook versions of this title. Owning the paper version of this book entitles you to purchase the electronic versions at a terrific discount.

PDFs are great for carrying around on your laptop—they are hyperlinked, have color, and are fully searchable. Most titles are also available for the iPhone and iPod touch, Amazon Kindle, and other popular e-book readers.

Buy now at *https://pragprog.com/coupon*

Contact Us

Online Orders:	*https://pragprog.com/catalog*
Customer Service:	*support@pragprog.com*
International Rights:	*translations@pragprog.com*
Academic Use:	*academic@pragprog.com*
Write for Us:	*http://write-for-us.pragprog.com*
Or Call:	+1 800-699-7764

Milton Keynes UK
Ingram Content Group UK Ltd.
UKHW010750160824
447011UK00008B/122